Bodies on t

by Trevor J

ORCHARD PUBLICATIONS
2 Orchard Close, Chudleigh, Devon TQ13 0LR
Telephone: (01626) 852714

ISBN 1 898964 63 7

Printed by
Hedgerow Print, Crediton, Devon EX17 1ES

CONTENTS

Introduction   2

1. A Princetown Tragedy   3

2. The Walton Howard Mystery   8

3. Dartmoor Prison Convicts   25

4. Deaths on Dartmoor Roads   32

5. Another Little Drink (A Miscellany)   40

6. Murder on Valentine's Day   46

7. Deadmans Bottom   54

8. Alone on the Moor   61

9. Mass Graves and other Prison Events   68

10. A Story of Three Lives   76

Introduction

The tales in this little book are not as gruesome as the title suggests. The author relates several events in Dartmoor's history among which are accounts of the dangers faced by miners who lived and toiled on the moor; the fate of two strangers who perished in unexplained circumstances; what the old time prison warders faced in charge of the most dangerous convicts in captivity; a murder, a suicide and roadside fatalities which are a continuing problem. These and several more incidents are linked by the demise of the characters associated with them.

The author respectfully dedicates this work to those who perished. May the innocent Rest In Peace and the sinners among them find forgiveness wherever they may lie.

These stories first appeared in the bi-monthly magazine *Dartmoor News* and are reproduced by agreement with the editor Mr. Paul Rendell.

A PRINCETOWN TRAGEDY

Did Clara Steal the Pigs?

Just days before Clara Kistle killed herself in May 1914 Harry Caunter, who occupied Bachelors Hall on the outskirts of Princetown, lost two pigs which he thought must have been stolen. His property was adjacent to the Oakery* where Clara, a forty two year old widow, carried on dairy farming after the death of her husband Edwin James Kistle. He was a stone mason and breeder of bullocks who died two years previously and was known locally as 'Gentleman Jim' because of his dapper appearance. His wife was left with four daughters and one son all under fourteen years of age. Three older daughters had jobs. The Kistle family were honest hard working members of the Princetown community and deeply religious. The events about to be described shocked the Dartmoor town and the tremors linger to this day among older residents, nearly all of whom are reluctant to talk about a heart-rending incident that occurred before they were born but which they remember being discussed years afterwards.

Harry Caunter looked for his missing pigs but without result so he reported their loss to the police. We now come to a critical point in our story, the events of Tuesday 12th May, 1914 when Clara allegedly went to Tavistock market and tried to sell a portion of pig meat (some accounts say it was half a pig). If true this was a strange thing for her to have done because market day at Tavistock was always Friday although there are and were then a number of small traders occupying premises around the Pannier Market building, some of them butchers. The journey there and back by horse and trap would have occupied several hours including the time required to offer her wares and possibly make a sale. Some time during the day a live pig was discovered in her shippen, probably during her absence. We do not know who found the animal or how its presence there became known, but that and the fact Clara had visited Tavistock with a portion of a pig for sale must have been brought to the attention of the police who visited Oakery that same evening and informed her she was under suspicion for stealing Harry Caunter's pigs. The two police officers who saw Clara, the resident Constable in Princetown PC Weekes and Tavistock Police Sergeant Screech, were afterwards unable

---

* The Kistle family home, now in ruins, stood in the little dell adjacent to the clapper which spans the Blackabrook on the Princetown – Two Bridges road and is known nowadays as the 'Ockery', but to the family who lived there it was always called 'Oakery'.

to agree what effect their visit had on her; one said she had been very distressed and the other said not. Whatever the case may have been Clara was taken ill that same night.

On Wednesday 13th May Clara Kistle sent a note (by what means is not clear) to Mr. Coaker of Sherberton near Hexworthy asking for help (the Kistle family were close friends of some of the Coakers). 'Mr. Coaker, will you be so kind as to come out? I am in great trouble. I have not a friend in the world and have five children to keep. It is about Harry Caunter's pigs. I will give you anything if you will come out, and you told me you would any time I was in trouble. C. Kistle. PS come out this morning please'. Either the note did not reach Mr. Coaker in time or for some reason he was unable to respond to this heartfelt plea. That same evening the police returned to Oakery with a search warrant. They found Clara in bed feeling unwell but able to get up for a short while (to assist them in the search perhaps) before going to bed again feeling ill. Nothing was found and the policemen left. Clara Kistle died in the early hours of the morning of Thursday 14th May 1914 having taken a lethal dose of arsenic.

An inquest was held at Princetown on Friday 15th May and adjourned until 22nd May to enable an analyst to check the dead woman's stomach contents for poison. Sufficient arsenic to cause death was found and at the resumed hearing the Coroner Mr. H.C. Brown accepted the jury's verdict of 'Suicide whilst temporarily insane'. The story created widespread publicity (not to mention the scandal and stigma which was cast on the Kistle family) for what seemed to be a clear case of theft and deceit by a poor widow struggling to support a large family amid hardship and poverty. Most people assumed Clara committed suicide in the aftermath of shame and remorse for her 'crime'. Until now.

A study of the evidence presented to the Coroner and other hitherto unknown family circumstances kindly provided by Clara's grandchildren (Joan Taber of Denver, Colorado, U.S.A. and the late Margery Harman of Southsea, Hants) not only casts doubt on what was assumed but implies another person or persons committed the act she was accused of. They have gathered an impressive amount of information which strongly suggests Clara was innocent.

Let us start with Clara's family who were all small in stature including the deceased who can best be described as slender and petite. Could such a woman venture out over the fields in the dark (the thief would hardly have risked taking them by day) and manage to drive two pigs on to her property?

If she had done the children would have known and one of them surely would have given the game away on being questioned. Pigs are noisy creatures especially when hungry and how were they to be fed? The shippen was on the other side of the Blackabrook River to the farmhouse and close to the road (it is there to this day). Did someone leave a pig there on the Tuesday in a panic, possibly because they were on the verge of being discovered? Who killed the other animal and where were the offal and other remains? The police searched the house on the evening of Wednesday 13th May and stated in evidence to the Coroner they 'searched the drawers'. The Coroner asked: 'Did you search the house?' Answer: 'No'. Coroner: 'Having regard to the turn things have taken it is a pity you did not do so'. It is a puzzle why the place wasn't more thoroughly searched. Was it because by now the police had other suspicions? Who found the pig and who informed the police? Was the discovery made whilst Clara was in Tavistock? These questions were never satisfactorily answered - the circumstantial evidence alone 'convicted' Clara Kistle of stealing Harry Caunter's pigs and killing one of them to sell.

Dr. C. Brodrick of Tavistock who performed a post mortem examination told the Coroner Clara's body was 'well nourished although thin'. With five young children to care for and a dairy farm to run her slimness was not surprising. The key phrase is 'well nourished' and this is reflected in the appearance of her children, all of whom were obviously healthy, clean and well dressed (see photo) even if they were photographed in their 'Sunday best' with frilled petticoats and lockets on display. They were not deprived or hungry but a well cared for family. Clara had a thriving stall at Tavistock market which attracted several good customers, and a regular delivery of her dairy products was made to the Deputy Governor at Dartmoor Prison. Her solicitors were Messrs. Chilcott and Chilcott of Tavistock. When she died her Post Office account stood at over £133 pounds, a considerable sum at that time, with Insurance yielding £36. Her property and farm stock was valued at more than £97 (the house was leasehold). Clara was solvent in every sense, running a modest but successful business, and able to enjoy little luxuries from time to time (the family know she often bought a tin of salmon to share with one of her older daughters when she visited from Taunton where she worked). Finally no family in Princetown was more liked and respected, a fact that was made evident many times when family members visited the town years later and were always warmly welcomed by those who knew them.

The Kistle children at the Oakery. Back row: Lillie, Ada, Minnie. Front row: May, Ivy, Frederick, Nellie. Sitting: Doris. (Courtesy Joan Taber)

Clara had no need to steal someone else's livestock. In any case it is extremely unlikely she would have done anything which might have compromised her family or risked losing her customers, not to mention her standing in the community. If times were hard she could have taken a lodger, there had been lodgers at the Oakery before and there was always a demand for accommodation. The key witness, a man who came to help with the milking, was not called to give evidence at the inquest. He would have been the first to spot a pig in the shippen. Did he report it to the police? Did he tell Clara on her return from Tavistock? Was it he or an accomplice who stole the pigs and compromised Clara by giving her a piece which perhaps she unwittingly accepted without realising it was stolen property? That would explain her appeal for help to Mr. Coaker. In any case would a guilty person make such a plea for help? I think not.

Whoever the culprit was their life could never afterwards have been a happy one with the knowledge that what was done resulted in such terrible consequences. Clara Kistle probably took the first dose of poison after the police questioned her on Tuesday evening in the aftermath of shock and horror at being accused of stealing. She was buried in Princetown Churchyard under the Burial Laws Amendment Act 1880 which meant that although she was a devout Christian, because she was a suicide she was denied a burial service. The Duchy of Cornwall landlords allowed her children to remain at the Oakery until arrangements could be made for their care. Nellie, who at

6

thirteen was the oldest of the children living at home, was taken in as one of the family by Samuel Perkins, Clara's brother, who was a Dartmoor Prison Warder and lived in prison accommodation with his family. Whatever happened he was anxious for the younger children to stay together and after much difficulty managed to get them accepted at the George Muller Orphanage in Bristol where, despite the good intentions of those in charge, their life lacked the love and kindness they had been used to. The Oakery was never lived in again and the house became derelict before being demolished some time around 1925.

The Policeman's View

Clara Kistle was more a victim of insensitive police investigation than she was of her feeling of shame. Here she was, a well-respected and devoutly Christian widow, bringing up her children against all the hardships so prevalent at that time. Her small business provided well for her and her family to such an extent that she had no reason to steal. The motives of necessity or greed could not seriously be considered and could she, a slightly built woman, have driven two pigs at night without causing any noise or suspicion? No.

The demands to detect crime placed upon a constable at that time were significant because an unsolved crime was a black mark against an officer's ability and therefore the methods adopted to investigate this matter might be somewhat questionable. 'Over zealous investigation' was not uncommon and the evidence of a proper enquiry in these circumstances is scant to say the least. Given the facts I would be very surprised indeed if Clara had been the offender. Unfortunately there are no surviving documents in the police archives relating to this matter, but in my view there are two victims in this tragic story. Mr Caunter was the victim of a petty thief but Clara Kistle was perhaps the greater victim of this very peculiar police investigation where too great a weight was put on the circumstantial evidence rather than motive and fact.

Constable Simon Dell, MBE., QCB.

Acknowledgements.
Kistle family descendants Joan Taber and the late Marjorie Harman.
P.C. Simon Dell MBE., QCB.
Mr. David Worth, Princetown.
Western Evening Herald. Totnes Times & Devon News.
Illustrated Western Weekly News.

THE STRANGE STORY OF WALTON HOWARD

A young man living with his parents in Warrington (Lancs.) bid them a fond farewell before returning to his lodgings in Bolton where he worked. He was expected home the following weekend but never arrived. Instead he packed a suitcase and immediately after leaving work the next Saturday disappeared without trace. Nothing was heard of him despite extensive police enquiries and appeals for information in the newspapers.

Ten weeks later a decomposed body was found on Dartmoor over 200 miles away and articles found on the body were identified as Walton Howard's, the missing son. But was it him? A wristwatch and a manicure set were the only identification and the physical appearance of the dead man was quite different from that of the missing man. At least one article of clothing was not his preference in tone or design. He did not know anyone in Devon

and the Dartmoor region was entirely unknown to him. The cause of death was never established and an inquest returned an open verdict.

What really happened? Was it Walton's body? If not, who was the unknown man buried in a pauper's grave with no name on the coffin? Then another man from Bolton is found dead in similar circumstances. Was it just coincidence? These chilling questions were never satisfactorily answered and are as baffling today as when they were first asked nearly seventy years ago. The events which caught the imagination of the nation and the people of Dartmoor in particular are examined here and provide a thought provoking narrative which will intrigue the reader, for without doubt this is the most extraordinary tale ever to emerge from southern England's 'Last Wilderness'.

The Story

Walton Howard (from 'The Corpse on the Moor' by Beatrice Chase).

Saturday 3rd November 1934 was a cold bleak day on the moor and farmer Jack Bailey of Higher Merripit Farm, Postbridge, decided to check over his cattle which were grazing on the slopes above the East Dart River. As he bent his head against the bitter wind, his dog's unusual behaviour caught Mr. Bailey's eye. It was worrying at something in the undergrowth. Thinking to find a dead animal he went to investigate and was 'taken aback' as he later put it to find the remains of a man. He immediately called the police and after they had finished their examination, helped carry the corpse off the moor to Postbridge where it was given into the care of Messrs. J.T. Halfyard, the Princetown undertakers.

On Monday 5th November the *Western Morning News* reported the find:

'The decomposed body of a man was on Saturday found lying in a bog at Roater Marsh* near Postbridge by Mr. Bailey, a farmer, who was looking for his cattle. How the man, whose identity is unknown, came by his death is a mystery. It is quite possible that he walked unknowingly into the bog, many of which exist on the moor, some to a considerable depth, and could not extricate himself. It is believed the body must have been at the spot, which is within a few miles of Princetown, for some considerable time. It is thought that the dead man was from 35 to 40 years of age. He was about 6ft. in height, of medium build, and had dark brown hair with, it is believed, a pointed beard. The fingernails were well manicured.

He was dressed in grey flannel trousers, a mauve coloured tweed jacket, and a grey tweed waistcoat. He also wore a recently soled pair of black shoes size 8 with rubber tips on the heels. They were marked 'Benefit' – evidently the name of the makers. Other articles of clothing were a brown trilby hat, bulldog make braces, blue tie with white spots, and one mauve and one blue silk handkerchief with floral designs. The sum of 4s 5d was found as well as a Swiss made wristlet watch with an illuminated dial but no hands. There was also a small brown leather wallet, and a manicure set in the shape of a pocket knife with a white and brown handle on which was the word 'Manicure'; a quarter size whisky bottle and a shoemaker's knife. Any information leading to the identity of the man would be gladly received by Tavistock Police'.

Other bodies have been found on Dartmoor from time to time, mostly of people caught in snowstorms, and nearly always 'locals' or those whose business is on the moor – farmers and the like. In 1853 three soldiers lost their lives in similar circumstances near Princetown – the grave of the Three

*Roater Marsh – the Devonshire vernacular for Rowtor or Rowter. The area is a wild and lonely place below the slopes of Row Tor, shown on some maps as Rough Tor.

Valiant Soldiers can be seen in the churchyard and their story is a familiar one in that locality (see page 64).

But for the Dartmoor Rescue Group there would undoubtedly be other tragedies among walkers· on the moor and the occasional suicides make poignant reading when they occur, but in nearly every case the victims have been moorland people or someone from the border towns. Therefore the Tavistock police who were in charge of the case concentrated their enquiries in the immediate neighbourhood. This time though they had no success. No-one had been reported missing. It was most strange.

Meanwhile an inquest had been held. The *Western Morning News* reported on Tuesday 6th November 1934:

'The mystery of how an unknown man came to be lying dead on Dartmoor was not revealed at an inquest which was opened at Postbridge yesterday by the Okehampton Coroner, Mr. H.C. Brown. There has been no response so far to the description of the man sent out by police, and medical evidence, owing to the state of the body, was unable to establish the cause of death. The Coroner adjourned the inquest in order to give the police a reasonable chance of establishing the man's identity.

Mr. John Henry Bailey said that on Saturday he was walking across the moor when he saw the dead body of a man. "At first I mistook it for the remains of an animal" he said, "it was lying in the swamp full length and it was obvious it had been there some time". The witness informed the police. He knew the spot well, it was always swampy even in the dry season. There was no path or track anywhere near. He had passed close to the place about six weeks before but he very likely did not see the body because it was not visible until one was within a few feet of it.

The Coroner: "Did you see anything near the body?" "I and a constable saw a knife There was no sign of a struggle and I could see where the man had laid before".

Sgt. Gale of Tavistock said he went with Constable Body of Mary Tavy to the place where Mr. Bailey had found the body. It appeared to be that of a man between 40 and 45 years of age. "About five yards away from the body on the ground I found a rusty cobbler's knife," said the Sergeant, producing the implement. "I also found a pencil, a quarter pint whisky bottle, the stopper of which was in the waistcoat pocket on the body. From the rushes it looked as if the man had laid near these things at first". He described the man's clothing and other articles which were found as previously reported. The two handkerchiefs were tied around the man's neck and knotted at the back.

"His right shoe was on his foot and had recently been soled, and the left one was found near the knife. There was some growth of beard on the man's chin and he had well manicured fingernails. I do not think he was of the tramp class, it appeared to be the body of a respectable man." he said.

The Coroner: "Was a stick found near the body?" "No". "You have circulated a description of the body?" "Yes, but up to now there has been no response". Dr. F.W.A. Watt of Tavistock said the condition of the body made it impossible to ascertain the cause of death. The Coroner: "There were no marks suggestive of a knife having been used?" "No". "You cannot say what was the cause of death?" "No. It is quite possible he died of exposure but there is nothing to show it". The Coroner said "I do not intend to close the inquest until the police have had a chance to identify the man and I will therefore adjourn it until December 27th. It occurs to me this man might have written to someone and said he was down and out, and or suggested suicide. I cannot understand if he was a tourist his being on the moor without a stick. Another alternative is that he might have got lost in a fog, but then, people do not choose a bog in which to lie down. He might have fainted perhaps".

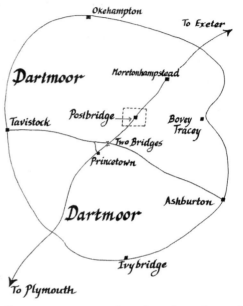

Dartmoor area showing location of Postbridge.

Dr. Watt also stated there was no direct evidence of any fracture of a limb, but of course one might have been sprained. The body will be buried at Postbridge today', the report went on, 'and photographs and fingerprints were taken last night.'

The local and national newspapers sensed a story and published the details of the case including an account of the funeral which took place on the same day as the Inquest. Several residents of the district who had read the news in the papers attended, despite the cruel weather, out of respect for the stranger and sympathy for his unknown family. The death certificate simply said 'Name Unknown'.

The service was exceptional in that the coffin had no nameplate or inscription of any kind but the proceedings were conducted with great reverence by the Rev. Stanhope Lovett of Princetown. Mr. Bailey was one of the bearers, the others being Police Constable Tucker of Princetown, Mr. R.D. Bolt, a well known Princetown resident, and Mr. J. Southcott of Postbridge.

To the lasting credit of local people floral tributes were not lacking. Sir Courtenay Bennett whose home (Archerton) was close to where the body was found sent a wreath of Flanders Poppies tied with black ribbon. A bunch of white chrysanthemums bore a card inscribed: 'With deepest sympathy to an unknown mother from a friend'. There was a posy placed anonymously on the grave by a Postbridge lady. Pride of place went to a large arrangement of golden chrysanthemums tied with blue ribbon from Miss Beatrice Chase (real name Katherine Parr) a well-known authoress who lived at Widecombe-in-the-Moor and whose sympathy was aroused through the newspaper reports.

Olive Katherine Parr was a direct descendant of William, Baron Kendal of Westmoreland, brother to Queen Katherine Parr of England (sixth and last wife of Henry VIII.). As 'Beatrice Chase' she was famous in her own right for her books about Dartmoor life which included *Through a Dartmoor Window* and *The Heart of the Moor.* The author John Oxenham bestowed on her the title 'My Lady of the Moor' as a tribute and in connection with his novel of that name. She was therefore a prominent figure on Dartmoor who took her title seriously – in fact it was this sense of duty which prompted her to attend the funeral.

In an account of it in the *Mid-Devon Advertiser* (November 10th 1934) she wrote: 'I felt as Lady of the Moor it was up to me to show the last act of respect and kindness in case his relatives were traced. There has not yet been time and if they do turn up they would feel dreadful about that funeral if there had not been one ray of light...' As we shall presently see she was to become actively involved in the later stages of this mysterious affair.

Miss Chase as I shall refer to her, afterwards commented how the little churchyard overlooked the heart of the moor and the very spot where the body was found. As dusk approached the sympathisers, about fifteen in number, dispersed leaving the stranger buried in a poor deal coffin under the moorland soil. Who was he? Where did he come from? Above all what on earth was he doing on Dartmoor in the cold of winter? Those questions might well be asked today because no satisfactory explanation ever came to light. All this time the police in far away Lancashire were doing their best to solve a mystery of their own – the disappearance of thirty one year old Walton Howard of Warrington. Mr. Howard, a single man, was a native of the town who worked as a foreman at Walkers Tannery in Bolton. He lodged there during the working week and at the weekends went to his parent's home in the Fearnhead area of Warrington. They last saw him on 19th August when he

Postbridge area where Walton's body was found.

said good-bye as he left for his Bolton lodgings. That was a Sunday evening. On the following Saturday, after finishing work at mid-day, he was seen wearing a brown suit and carrying a suitcase, with a raincoat over his arm as if about to go on a journey. It was afterwards established he had drawn £10 from his bank account, a fairly large sum for those days. He then vanished without trace and without a word to his mother and father. Of course the alarm was soon raised (he was their only son whom they had late in life) and a police investigation began which extended over an ever widening area but without result. Mr. and Mrs. Howard advertised extensively in the local and national newspapers, offering a reward for information of any kind and pleading for their son to contact them. The response to all their efforts was an uncanny silence.

The only explanation they could think of was a loss of memory. Mr. Howard later recalled that Walton had accompanied them on holiday to Llandudno in June that year when the weather had been terribly hot and he got badly burnt by the sun as he watched a cricket match (Walton was a keen sportsman who followed rugby and cricket with enthusiasm). After that they noticed he became much quieter and spent a lot of time indoors. Perhaps it had affected his brain or maybe he banged his head at work, which was the opinion of the men at the tannery. Head injuries were an occupational hazard in the part of the works he was responsible for where hides were hung for long periods during the curing process. His obvious intention of going away pointed to a premeditated decision and was completely out of character.

The police twice asked the BBC in Manchester and London to broadcast an appeal for information but this was refused as the Corporation's policy at this time was to limit this type of message to cases where a relative had a serious illness. As a last resort the Chief Constable decided to put out an 'All Stations' alert and a circular was sent to every police force in the country with Walton's particulars and description. It was supplemented with a photograph.

The first clue however came from an unexpected source and never was the power of the media demonstrated more dramatically than in this instance. The details of the Dartmoor tragedy were reported by several daily papers one of which, the *Daily Mail*, listed the objects found on the body. It was read by a close neighbour of the Howard family who thought there could be a link with the finding of a leather worker's knife and who knew Walton possessed a manicure set like the one described in the report. She took the paper to Mrs. Howard who read it with dread, unwilling to believe her son could have wandered as far afield as Dartmoor which she said 'They had only read about in books'. She did recognise the items that were found and told the Warrington police who in turn contacted their colleagues in Devon requesting that they be sent to them for identification. The Tavistock police thought it unlikely that the man they sought could have come from so far away but finally the articles were sent and poor Mrs. Howard saw at once they belonged to her Walton. The manicure set had been a present from her and the watch had a distinctive mark inside the casing which was recognised

PERSONAL.

" MISSING. £10 REWARD.—Walton Howard. 31 years. Grove House. Fearnhead. Warrington. Last seen in Bolton noon Saturday. August 25. 5ft. 10½in. Fresh complexion. wavy hair, military bearing. Brownish new mixture suit. soft hat, carrying light raincoat. brown suitcase containing light grey suit, other clothing. Thought sudden loss memory following exposure to July sun on holiday. Possibly wandered south. £10 paid for definite information leading to recovery. Should this reach his notice and understanding, write home at once."

Mr. and Mrs. Howard's plea for news of their missing son.

14

by a local watch repairer who had done some work on it and left his personal stamp inside. The ten weeks of agony for the Howards was over but it was not a straightforward solution to the case by any means.

Our story now shifts back to Dartmoor where the papers had announced the dead man came from Warrington and had been identified. No details were given and Miss Beatrice Chase, who was of Lancashire descent and possessed an extremely sympathetic nature (she did charity work in London's East End in her younger days to the detriment of her health) got in touch with the Howards with the help of the Chief Constable of the county. Her letter to them indicates her concern:

'Beatrice Chase, Venton House, Widecombe-in-the-Moor, Newton Abbot, Devon. 10th November 1934

I cannot begin this letter in the ordinary way because I do not know to whom I am writing. The paper just says 'relatives'. But I do not want to lose a day in trying to send you some comfor. I send a picture of my Chapel* where your son's name is enshrined in the Book of the Dead and daily prayers have been offered for him since Monday and will continue. I have prayed many times a day for his relatives...I am a Roman Catholic and he was buried by a Church of England Vicar from Princetown...if you come at any time to visit his grave please let me know and please visit me. God Bless You and Comfort You.

     Yours devotedly,
     Katherine Parr (Beatrice Chase)'.

A lasting friendship resulted from this correspondence and Miss Chase performed a noble gesture by retrieving her chrysanthemums from the grave and forwarding them to Walton's parents. In a letter of thanks Mrs. Howard said: 'The wonderful kindness of the moorland people in attending the burial fills our hearts with gratitude. In that bitter weather they followed our boy to that lonely grave. We can only thank them...and bless them in our hearts for ever'.

Some idea of their terrible loss and the loving bond they shared with their son is revealed in this further extract from Mrs. Howard's letter: '...words cannot tell you of our pain and grief. He was our one beloved son, cherished all his life, loving us and his home as we loved him. For the past five years he has been engaged at Bolton, coming home for weekends, and from there

---

*She had a private chapel which was built to her specifications adjacent to her house. It still stands.

he disappeared. No reason can be given, probe as we may…he was sought after far and wide in advertisement and police enquiries but to no avail.'

A lady who as a girl lived next door to the Howard family confirmed to the author they were a highly respected and religious family, were regular churchgoers and that Walton was a clean living, industrious and sober young man. Here we may pause to consider why an upright young fellow from a respectable family, bought up in a middle class home, should suddenly and deliberately go away. He had a good job, money in the bank, and substantial sums invested in his name. He had an abiding affection for his parents yet no attempt was made to contact them or reassure them in any way. How and why did he go to Postbridge where he knew no-one and had no reason to be? Beatrice Chase also contemplated these things and was intrigued by them but the strangest thing of all was the receipt of a photograph of their son sent to her by Mrs. Howard.

She happened to show it to one of the policemen who had helped remove the body from the moor and his immediate comment was: 'That's not the man we found'. This new twist to the tale caused much consternation. If it wasn't Walton Howard, then who was it? The possibility arose that enquiries might have to be resumed and what if his belongings turned out to be stolen? The reader will recall that when he was last seen Walton was wearing a brown suit and carried a raincoat and a suitcase. The body on the moor was dressed quite differently and there was no raincoat or suitcase found at the scene. In fact they were never found. In addition the man's age had been estimated to be firstly (when found) thirty five to forty and then (at the first inquest) forty to forty five. He was bearded. Walton was only thirty one and clean shaven. The body was described as having dark brown hair; his was very fair. Ironically, the Tavistock police received the 'All Stations' circular the very day the body was found and it asked them to look out for a completely different man!

This was not all. After comparing the circular picture with the one Mrs. Howard had sent, Miss Chase and the policeman she had spoken to agreed there was no likeness. A bizarre feature came to light concerning the circular photo: it had been supplied by a friend with whom Walton had shared his lodgings and not by the family. Mrs. Howard said she and her husband never saw that particular picture and furthermore her son 'hated spotted ties' and would never have worn one (the picture evidently depicted a man wearing such a tie and the body had a blue tie with white spots when found). Then a dramatic new story broke which intensified everyone's bewilderment.

Only fourteen days after Walton Howard's possessions were identified another man was found dead, this time at the foot of the cliffs at Beachy Head. All the indications were that he had fallen over the cliff which was about 500ft. high at that point. The amazing thing was that when he was finally identified it was learned that he too came from Bolton (from where Walton Howard had disappeared). This was not all for the man was wearing a brown suit, a trilby hat was found nearby, and his watch had the minute hand missing. The similarities in the two deaths are at once apparent. Add to this the fact that both men had one shoe lying beside them when they were found and that they carried no documents of any kind which might have identified them and the impression is strong that there was more than coincidence at work.

On 1st December 1934 the *Eastbourne Chronicle* stated:

'The man whose body was found at the foot of the cliffs at Beachy Head on Saturday was the subject of an Inquest opened by the East Sussex Coroner Dr. E. F. Hoare at the Town Hall on Tuesday. Adjourning the inquest for a fortnight, the Coroner said there was no evidence as to who the man was or how he came to fall over the cliff. Medical evidence detailed the body's many injuries. Death was due to the shock of the injuries, obviously sustained by a fall and subsequent immersion in the sea. The injuries were sufficient to account for the death but any chance of recovery the man might have had were destroyed by partial drowning.

Mr. Arthur Ball of Dennis Road said that at 9.15am on Saturday he was walking on the beach about 500 yards west of the lighthouse when he saw a man lying face downwards on the beach. He was dead and had evidently fallen over the cliff. He appeared to be between forty and forty five years of age and was slightly bald with dark hair. He wore a brown suit and there was a trilby hat nearby. A police sergeant described how he examined the body: 'The minute hand of the man's watch was missing...there was a silver cigarette case bearing the initials G.M. ...there were no letters or documents of any kind' .

As Beatrice Chase pointed out: 'These are details no writer could invent. They are too mad to be anything but true'. She acquainted the Eastbourne police with the several similarities to the Dartmoor case. It was discussed from many angles but nothing was done. She was convinced there must be some connection between the two deaths. As in the Walton Howard affair there were several questions to which no answer could be given. The final inquest revealed further similarities.

From the *Eastbourne Gazette* 19th December 1934:

'The inquest on the man who was found dead on the rocks below Beachy Head on November 24th was closed on Monday when the Coroner returned a verdict of "Found Dead". The inquest had been adjourned for the identification of the man. The coroner said he had been identified by his brother as George Miller, aged 31, an unemployed ship's steward of Bolton. The brother had no idea why Miller was in Eastbourne. The coroner said he had found no further information as to how or why the man came to be in the position in which he was discovered. "There is not sufficient evidence to show how this man came to get over the cliff" he said "whether it was accidental or suicidal. Although there is a grave suspicion of suicide about it there is nothing definite and I think he should be given the benefit of the doubt". The *Eastbourne Chronicle* added these details: 'A man named Leslie Miller identified the body as that of his brother, George Miller, aged 31, of Minister Road, Bolton'.

Thus the Eastbourne case closed but consider the astounding similarities to the Dartmoor tragedy. Both men:

Were at first thought to be forty to forty five years old and were actually thirty one.

Had one or more hands missing from their watches.

Had one shoe off and found lying close to them.

Had trilby hats.

Disappeared from Bolton.

Had no reason to be in the places where they died.

Carried no identification.

Had brown suits.

Were given the benefit of the doubt concerning possible suicide and had what amounted to the same verdict recorded at their Inquests.

George Miller: 'Found Dead'. Walton Howard: 'Open verdict'.

Were these merely coincidental? Did they know one another? Are their deaths linked in any way? Was identification deliberately concealed? Was there a sinister meaning in the damaged watches and the loose shoes? What did Mr. and Mrs. Howard think? Their thoughts, if any, are not recorded although Miss Chase must have acquainted them with the details. The truth of it cannot now be ascertained and forensic science was in its infancy then otherwise more illuminating details might have been revealed.

Mr. and Mrs. Howard were treated with great kindness when they came to Devon for the inquest on their son. Beatrice Chase received them at her home in Widecombe and being a deeply religious woman was able to comfort them in prayer. She afterwards took them to see the grave and saw them to their hotel. Mr. Bailey walked with them the same afternoon to the spot where the body was found.

Postbridge Village Hall was the venue for the resumed inquest which opened at 2.00pm on 10th January 1935. It had been postponed by an understanding coroner because the original date (27th December) would have caused great inconvenience to the parents who would have had to leave home before Christmas and spend those days away from home in order to attend. They were of course the chief witnesses. Mrs. Lizzie Mary Harriet Howard confirmed her recognition of the wallet, manicure set and watch as belonging to her son. She described his last departure from home and told of their search for news of him. On Sunday 19th August he had left home to return to Bolton. 'We saw him to the door and he kissed me and said goodbye to his father and his father patted him on the shoulder and said "take care of yourself my boy and God Bless You". She knew of no love affairs, there were no quarrels and she was sure he had no enemies. He was practically a teetotaller.

Mr. William Stubbs Howard, a retired corporation official, said he and his son were on terms of greatest affection. 'He had no worries, financial or otherwise. He had money saved in the bank, money invested in his own name, and I used to help him every month' (Walton was a foreman in the 'belly sheds' – the official name for that part of the tannery – the title is self explanatory. He was the lowest grade of foreman in the works and not well paid). 'A better boy never lived,' continued Mr. Howard 'he was industrious, honourable and sober'. He broke down whilst giving evidence saying: 'His mother and I have practically lived for the boy'. When asked if his son might have committed suicide or ever threatened to do so Mr. Howard emphatically declared: 'Oh dear no! There was no possibility of it'.

A fellow employee at Messrs. Walkers Tannery, Mr. Henry Blundell of Bolton, said that Walton was always happy at his work. He last saw him at 12.20pm on Saturday 25th August carrying a suitcase. It was the last known sighting.

The coroner referred to the knife and the whisky bottle found lying beside the corpse. Tests carried out on the knife proved negative he said. The whisky bottle showed traces of cresylic acid (disinfectant) but so dilute he could not believe it was a significant factor (it was afterwards learned that the constables at the scene had poured a weak solution of disinfectant over the body before searching it and the whisky bottle top found in the waistcoat pocket was then screwed back on. This could have accounted for the contamination.*The analyst's report on the contents showed no more than one part per 100,000 acid to water.

The coroner remarked: 'I do not feel justified in assuming deceased had destroyed himself'. The cause of death was unknown and the body was too decomposed to form an opinion as to the cause of death. Although he held a Home Office order for exhumation, the pathologist had advised no useful purpose would be served and accordingly an 'Open Verdict' was recorded.

What sort of man was Walton Howard? We have learned from the evidence of his parents how dutiful, affectionate and honourable he was. The neighbours too regarded him a clean living and highly respectable young chap. This view was endorsed by a lady who lived close by the Howard family and knew them well. She told me 'They were a very religious family, Walton attended church regularly with his parents and in fact obtained his first tannery job through church friends'. She also said how he was admired for the way in which he unashamedly wore his overalls when leaving home for the tannery; it was very much a 'middle class' area where he lived and it was a brave thing to do. His father was affectionately known as 'Gas' Howard, the author was told by another person who knew them, on account of his having been manager of the Corporation Gas Works. The same gentleman, now in his eighties and living on the South Coast was nevertheless amazed to hear that Walton was a workman and later a foreman at the tannery. 'With his background I would have thought he was at least being groomed for higher management' he said.

Walton's colleagues at Walkers Tannery recognised he was 'well to do'. He was well spoken (not having a local accent) and carried himself in an upright manner such that a casual observer might easily conclude of him 'there goes a soldier'. As a Grammar School boy he won prizes three years running which earned him compliments from his teachers. He afterwards had the drive and initiative to go to the local Technical Institute where he gained several first class certificates for tannery work.

The picture that emerges is of a model son, almost too good to be true.

*The author was told by a former tannery consultant (who, by the way, knew Walton Howard) that cresylic acid was used extensively in the trade as a mould inhibitor.

I do not doubt for a moment that the opinion of his neighbours and workmates were honestly held but Walton was a paradox in at least one respect and perhaps this was the clue to his behaviour. Some men at Walkers noticed less attractive traits in his character: a superior attitude tinged with contempt for the 'peasant workers'. Tannery work was a tough trade and maybe some of the men gave him a 'rough ride' in retaliation. Perhaps this affected him but the suspicion must arise that he was a paradox in other ways. Consider: a respectable and upright young man who is expected at home suddenly and without warning decides to go away. There can be no question it was his intention to journey somewhere. A man does not draw funds from his bank, pack a suitcase, leave work on a Saturday morning with a raincoat and go away unintentionally. A sudden loss of memory does not explain such an act. His departure I suggest was premeditated and timed to the minute. Why? Was he rejected in love after all? Did he lead a secret life in Bolton? Were there other reasons for his departure – did someone threaten to reveal something he did not wish his family to know about? With greatest respect to family and friends these questions inevitably arise in contemplating the reason for his swift and inexplicable disappearance.

The lady who knew the family so well (but does not wish to be identified) says that although the advertisements in the papers appealing for information suggested he may have 'wandered south', in fact it was the last place they expected he might go – Llandudno or Scarborough were more likely by far. Why then did he end up on a remote part of Dartmoor where he had never been and knew no-one? I suggest it was·because it was the very last place he would be sought after. He wanted to disappear and he chose the ideal location. Dartmoor then was still a remote place and Postbridge is situated almost exactly in the centre of its wildest parts. In the age before mass motoring it was not an easy place to get to. Visitors to Dartmoor arrived by train and proceeded by bus or taxi to the upland towns and villages. Postbridge was served by Devon General buses which ran once a day from Exeter to Princetown, passing through the village en route. The alternative was by taxi. Why was Walton not remembered when police enquiries were later made? He was an outstanding man physically, tall, military bearing, strong featured and well spoken – the 'soldier type' it was said.

I believe that for most of the time he was missing he was already lying dead at the spot where he was found. He vanished in the last week of August when the undergrowth and bracken are lush and green. At the end of October and the first weeks of November (when he was found) the bracken dies, turns a golden brown and crumbles away. Likewise the undergrowth fades and dies and this was when his poor emaciated remains were finally exposed. On Mr. Bailey's own admission he could have passed by previously and not seen him. He also confided to Miss Chase that a young lady rode her pony across that part of the moor regularly without seeing him. The fact that the police did not have an accurate description and that Walton was missing for ten weeks could explain how there was no recollection of him by those who were questioned.

Where did he change his clothes? Where did he sleep? Where did he obtain further funds? Did he pawn or sell his raincoat and suitcase together with the contents? If he went to his bank and arranged a withdrawal it would have betrayed his whereabouts. Many a desperate man has dropped out of sight and even faked death in order to disappear. Could Walton have been such a man? Maybe his things were stolen or he gave them away and maybe it was another person who was found. There are several discrepancies between the description of the dead man and what we know of Walton. He had fair hair – the dead man's hair was dark brown. There was a vast difference between the estimated age of the corpse (forty to forty five) and Walton Howard's real age, thirty one. The body had a beard – Walton did not. Then again, a pointed beard (as reported in the finding of the body) suggest it was groomed. It also suggests a disguise. Could Walton have dyed his hair? We will not now ever know the truth of it but assuming it was his body on that desolate marsh we may fairly conclude:

His departure was calculated and deliberate.

He went south and west where he knew he would be least suspected of going.

Somehow he found himself in Postbridge, probably by chance – or was it? By another amazing coincidence two families who were on holiday in the vicinity were from Fearnhead too, although they did not know the Howard family. Could Walton by chance have heard of their destination and decided it would be a good place to go? He died alone on the moor and lay undiscovered for several weeks. If he did not take his own life the mental anguish he must have endured miles away from family and friends can but evoke an overwhelming pity and sadness for him.

The police found a pencil – did he write a farewell note? Did he use the knife on himself? What was in the whisky bottle? Was it cresylic acid or the original contents? His mother testified to the coroner he was 'practically teetotal'. Was it therefore obtained to give him the 'Dutch courage' he might have needed? Was there an Eastbourne connection? Were both deaths suicide?

A lifetime later we may still ask was it really Walton Howard who was found? The late Mr. W. Halfyard of Princetown, a sprightly and compassionate man in his eighties when I spoke to him, told me he had made the very coffin the body was buried in and that he could verify many of the facts in this story. As for the man's identity: 'The explanation is probably very simple,' he said 'because when a person dies their body cells, hair for example, remain active for a time. Mr. Howard had lain on the moor for many days – weeks even – prior to being found. If he was clean shaven when he died it's more than likely his beard grew sufficiently to disguise his face. In fact I heard afterwards the police shaded in a beard over the photo Mrs. Howard sent – and there he was! He was recognised at once!'

The balance of evidence favours the opinion that it was indeed Walton Howard who was found dead. But just suppose it was someone else (and the same evidence does at least suggest the possibility) then who was it? All the questions relating to Walton would have to be raised concerning the unknown stranger. An entirely new mystery would present itself – what happened to Walton Howard? Did he live to a ripe old age in obscurity? Surely not – yet it is possible. We will never know.

What is certain is that his parents spent the rest of their lives wondering about the manner of his death and very unhappy years they were. The family are reunited now in Warrington cemetery. Walton (and I like to think it was him for his parent's sake) was exhumed shortly after the inquest and taken home for reburial. In due course he was joined by his father and in September 1945 by his mother. The parents' coffins each contained half of a divided bunch of carefully dried and pressed flowers – the chrysanthemums which were placed on their son's first grave by Beatrice Chase. The final word must go to the Coroner who said: 'This case will remain another mystery of Dartmoor'. He might well have added 'and of Warrington'.

The Policeman's View

I am not entirely convinced by the apparent coincidences in this case. Walton was a man who seemed to have no reason for disappearing, yet all the evidence points to him making plans to achieve anonymity.

The coincidence of Miller being found in similar circumstances is too much. If the offcers investigating this matter had the benefits of DNA testing, this would have at least identified Walton's body, but would not have solved the riddle of why his body lay in a marsh on Dartmoor.

Walton was wearing unfamiliar clothing - was this some elaborate plan to disguise himself? Was he running from something he felt was shameful, perhaps an illicit affair with Miller? Could he have actually been lodging with Miller at the time? Could Miller have been blackmailing Walton in order to get at his wealth? Perhaps they came down to Dartmoor together but things went terribly wrong resulting in Miller murdering Walton. Could Miller have disposed of the body in circumstances which would leave the body unidentifable? Whatever happened we are left with one of Dartmoor's greatest 20th century mysteries - a mystery which all the police investigative powers of today could not answer.

Constable Simon Dell, MBE., QCB.

Acknowledgements.
The Corpse on the Moor by Beatrice Chase (out of print).
Western Morning News (Plymouth).
Mid-Devon Advertiser (Newton Abbot).
Constable Simon Dell MBE., QCB.
Mr J. Marcus Harrison (Bolton) former colleague of Walton Howard.
Mr G. Roberts (Bournemouth) former Warrington resident.
Mr J.A. Hamlet (Warrington) ex - tannery employee.
The Strange Story of Walton Howard by Trevor James was first published in *Secret Devon* (Bossiney Books, Launceston, Cornwall 1994).
Maps drawn by artist Felicity Young and reproduced by kind permission of Bossiney Books.

DARTMOOR PRISON CONVICTS
(Relating to the period before 1900).

At the rear and to the right of the Church of St. Michaels and All Angels in Princetown are rows of small stone tablets inscribed with the dates and initials of convicts who died on the moor. They lie in a separate burial plot and the memorial stones relate only to those who were buried after 1902. Those who were interred between 1850 (when the convict prison opened) and 1902 lie in unmarked graves in the same area and their combined memorial takes the form of a simple granite cross erected in 1912. It stands close to the church tower and is a prominent feature of the churchyard. There are two separate headstones, one of which is another standard stone tablet which can be seen just in front of the cross in memory of a 'Borstal Boy' (of whom a number were sent to Dartmoor from Parkhurst after World War Two). The other is a traditional headstone in front of the rows of convict graves. It was placed there by the family of: 'L.D.C. who died February 2nd 1877. My Jesu Mercy'. It is the only memorial provided by a convict's family.

How did these men die? Most of them died of natural causes — pneumonia and related chest complaints (the notoriously wet Dartmoor weather and damp cells were a contributory factor); dropsy (known as oedema today) and often associated with a poor diet. Other killer diseases were influenza, typhus (gaol fever) and a brief outbreak of cholera. There were a number of suicides (a sad feature of prison life to this day).

The prison blocks we see now are replacement buildings for the original 'French' prisons built during the Napoleonic Wars, a number of which were pulled down towards the end of the 19th. century. The new blocks were built on the foundations by convict labour supervised by artisan warders. As in construction work today several men were accidentally killed, mostly by falling from scaffolding. The main body of prisoners were put to work quarrying and breaking stones, farming or digging the vast areas of bog and heath and draining it for cultivation. New arrivals were examined by the prison doctor and if pronounced fit did their stint working in the open under arduous conditions before being considered for lighter duties within the prison, tailoring for example, boot making, work in the kitchens and bake house, etc.

In June 1875 there was a fatal accident where you would least expect it. A convict gang were clearing the moor of boulders prior to digging. This was done by securing the stones with chains or ropes and man-hauling them away after undermining them by excavating under one side. The man who died was Frederick Whittey aged fifty one serving a prison sentence for forgery. He was the foremost man when the ground gave way without warning and he fell into the cavity which was only two feet deep. The stone, over a ton in weight, toppled onto him crushing him beneath it. He was extricated in minutes but died from severe internal injuries.

There were hazards within the prison. The main chimney stack (since demolished) had a number of flues connected to it which had to be cleaned periodically. One of them conveyed exhaust gases from the bakehouse and convict John Cummings was sent in one day in October 1882 to prepare for a cleaning machine to be inserted. A look-out man watched his progress (Cummings carried a light, presumably a lantern) but after a quarter of an hour he lost contact with him and the alarm was raised. The unfortunate man had performed his task but on the return trip he entered the wrong flue where a fire was burning and was overcome by the fumes. A rescue party of convicts found him but were beaten back by the fumes and the fire had to be reduced before they were able to recover his body. He was thirty two years of age and had spent nearly all his life in prison since his first conviction at the age of ten.

Convicts attempting to escape were shot at. The guards for the outside work parties were

Memorial cross for convicts who died before 1902 (Author's photo)

armed with Snider rifles with smooth bores designed to fire buckshot, but the guns were not loaded and if someone tried to run for it a cartridge had to be inserted from an ammunition pouch by which time an escapee could be a fast disappearing target. Nevertheless several convicts who tried to abscond were hit and killed whilst many more were severely wounded which prompted questions in the House of Commons about the number of men 'shot down like Jack-rabbits' at Dartmoor.

A classic example occurred on Christmas Eve 1896 when a work party was returning to the prison early as a thick mist closed in. Three men had planned to run away and they supposed now was the time to make their break. The ringleader was twenty two year old William Carter who was just starting a twelve year sentence for robbery with violence. The other two were burglars Ralph Goodwin and John Martin. As they approached a fir

Convict work party assembling (Courtesy Brian Jones)

plantation which offered cover for their escapade they threw handfuls of earth into the faces of the guards and ran. The Civil Guard escort, who were responsible for security outside the prison, opened fire and young Carter was killed on the spot. Martin was soon caught and overpowered whilst Goodwin, who got away, was recaptured in Plymouth two days later. The warders were punished if someone in their charge escaped and although the instructions laid down for use of firearms stipulated they should always aim low (to disable a fugitive not kill him) in the flurry of agitation and necessary haste the shooting was often erratic. An Inquest was always held when someone died at Dartmoor prison and in cases like this the jury, who were drawn from local people including fellow prison employees, always returned a verdict of 'Justifiable Homicide'. Any other conclusion would have resulted in a charge of manslaughter against the individual concerned.

Before the reader judges the issue too harshly it should be remembered attacks upon warders by convicts with the tools they were issued with – spades, crowbars, hammers, picks, etc. - were regular occurrences and it was a miracle no-one was killed. As it was several officers had to leave the service as a result of their injuries. The following examples will help in understanding what the old-time warders had to face.

It was November 1880 and the prison quarry was to witness a convict death during an escape attempt in the aftermath of violence and mutiny. Dartmoor Prison had recently received into custody some of Britain's worst offenders all serving not less than five years for the most heinous crimes imaginable. Among them was James Bevan a thirty five year old carpenter serving twenty five years. He and five other men had broken into an old lady's home and subjected her to torture culminating in placing her on the fire in order to make her tell them where she kept her money. They stole £180 from the house and left her for dead in a ditch. Bevan and two of his accomplices were convicted and sent to Taunton Prison. Their threatening behaviour on the train was so vicious the warders guarding them asked for a police constable to join them at Taunton station for the remainder of the journey. They were classed as 'very desperate men' and Bevan was later transferred to Portland where he was singled out as being 'a very shrewd, dangerous character and one who should be well looked after'. Then he was sent to Dartmoor.

Before long Bevan was planning to escape from the prison quarry where he worked and inciting others to do the same. Friday 3rd November 1880 saw an increase in the number of guards, the authorities having been informed something was brewing. In the afternoon Warder Lord warned Principle Warder John Westlake there was muttering among the men in his gang and he suspected there would soon be trouble. As a thick fog was developing it was decided to cease work and the men were told to hand in their tools prior to being marched back to the prison. It was then that Bevan attacked Mr. Westlake hitting him on the side of the head with the 'jumper' he used in his work (this was a thick iron bar with pointed ends used for making holes in granite blocks during the splitting process). Westlake fell and was again struck with the bar this time on his arm but managed to draw his sword to

Two old time Warders (Courtesy the late Mr. C. Waycott)

defend himself. The penalty for assaulting a warder was corporal punishment with the 'cat o' nine tails' or the birch rod and perhaps it was with this in mind that Bevan decided now was the time to give the signal for what was evidently a pre-planned mass escape. 'Now boys, come on – you promised you would' he yelled as he sprinted away. At the same time a warder exclaimed 'there's one off!' followed by shouts to the fleeing man to stop. One other convict took off after Bevan, a man called O'Brien, before shots were fired. Bevan staggered and fell dead. O'Brien was discovered lying on his back badly wounded. It was the very quick response of the guards which discouraged the other convicts from taking off after the pair who were shot. The post-mortem examination on the deceased revealed he had been hit by several slugs (each cartridge held thirteen 'shots') one of which one had penetrated the sac enclosing the heart and this was the fatal wound. 'Justifiable Homicide' was the verdict at the inquest later held.

Note. The Secretary of State's written instructions decreed:

1.	Sentries will allow no prisoner to escape, using their arms if necessary to enforce their orders.
2.	They are required to render immediate assistance in the event of an officer being assaulted….making use of their arms if necessary.

These requirements were never more effectively adhered to than in an incident that happened only two years later. Convict William Murray was only twenty three years old but had served six prison sentences and his conduct at Dartmoor was described as 'bad'. He had been punished for stealing other men's rations, fighting, assaulting an officer, using threatening and abusive language, and throwing dirt at an officer.

In November 1882 he was one of a party of convicts excavating sand from a pit at the rear of the Princetown Church with Warder John Kelly in charge. Another gang under Warder Edward Cole were working a short distance away. Murray had been reprimanded before dinner that day and when work resumed in the afternoon he stood idle when the rest of the men started digging. When Warder Kelly asked: 'Murray, are you going to work?' he started using abusive and disgusting language. Seizing a pick and swinging it over his head he shouted: 'You **** I will do for you.' After more threats he dropped the pick and grabbed a spade to use as a weapon. Warder Kelly now put a cartridge into his rifle as Murray got onto higher ground in defiant mood saying 'Shoot you ****' and 'I'll do for you' etc. Then he started throwing stones at Mr. Kelly hitting him several times. The rest of the men were ordered to fall in and prepare to march off when Murray called: 'Stand like **** men. I will do for the **** before he leaves here'.

Escape!

Meanwhile Warder Cole began escorting both gangs away from the scene. Mr. Kelly now had his rifle at the 'charge' and was advancing towards Murray who retreated backwards still throwing stones and mouthing defiance. A stone struck the warder on the head and as he fell back against a bank the prisoner jumped on top of him and grabbed the barrel of his rifle in an attempt to wrest it from him. The gun went off just as Warder Cole, who had been watching, fired to protect his comrade. Murray fell crying 'Oh Mr. Kelly, forgive me for what I have done' and 'let me die, let me die'. He was carried to the prison hospital where he died later that afternoon.

It was never established which rifle was responsible for Murray's death but the post-mortem revealed the buckshot wounds were all in the lower abdomen and legs, the fatal wound being a shot which perforated the pelvic artery resulting in death from loss of blood. Warder Cole therefore must have aimed low as per the instructions and acted perfectly in accordance with the necessity to open fire to protect a fellow officer. As the Coroner remarked at the Inquest: 'If Warder Kelly had been killed by the gun going off without Warder Cole having fired, he (Cole) would have been guilty of dereliction of duty'.

The Policeman's View

If we looked at these incidents using today's standards we might be well justified in considering the official sanctioning of shooting escaping convicts as brutal and archaic. Today's standards and emphasis on rehabilitation and resettlement were unheard of in those harsh days and when a prisoner took the decision to escape he did so knowing the risks involved.

Over the last twenty years I have been involved in numerous convict hunts where the greatest risk to the prisoner was a loss of remission – a small penalty compared to one hundred years ago. The escapee, however, still represents a serious risk to those pursuing him and I have on a few occasions been on the receiving end of a few well-aimed blows from some of them. Even so, I have never considered that even in those harsh Victorian days, the shooting of an escaping convict could be justified. Perhaps I'm just too soft but in contrast I can't help thinking that we should never judge those before us by using today's standards. Let us instead be grateful that we have come a long way since those dark ages and accept that these things are in the past and need to be used as lessons for the future. I am often asked why I am so interested in history – my reply has always been: "He who ignores history is condemned to re-live it". This small piece of history at Dartmoor Prison represents a significant lesson to the whole penal system.

Constable Simon Dell, MBE., QCB.

Acknowledgements.
Constable Simon Dell MBE., QCB.
Mr. David Worth, Princetown.
Tavistock Gazette.
The Criminal by Basil Thomson.
There's One Away by Trevor James.

DEATHS ON DARTMOOR ROADS

The surge in tourism on Dartmoor together with commercial and residential developments, particularly at Princetown, have resulted in a huge increase in traffic. Prison staff commute on a daily basis and the High Moorland Visitor Centre attracts more than 100,000 visitors annually. There are shops, cafes, and pubs and a busy Primary School. Public transport is sparse so cars and commercial vehicles constitute the traffic particularly in the Plymouth direction.

Regular drivers on Dartmoor constantly come across dead sheep, cattle and ponies as a result of collisions with motor vehicles. Rabbits, foxes and badgers are even more commonplace – even working dogs (collies) have been among the casualties. Sometimes people are killed.

Young Andrew Law was a talented student at Tavistock College who had already been offered a place at Loughborough University. He was a gifted rugby player who, in addition to playing for the college First Team, had represented Devon in the under fifteens and under sixteens and was a member of Tavistock Rugby Club. He played the cornet for Tavistock Junior Band. A talented swimmer, he held a Gold Award for Lifesaving and reached the Regional Finals in a cookery competition. As if all this were not enough in a busy life he had a part-time job at a hotel close to his Princetown home. Andrew also rode a motorcycle and was often observed by this writer as a considerate careful rider.

On New Years Eve 1997 he set off on his motorbike to meet friends in Tavistock and at about 9.00pm as he approached Merrivale Bridge a pony emerged from a farm gateway directly into his path. With no time to brake or take evasive action Andrew collided with the animal and was thrown off his bike into the path of a car going in the opposite direction. Despite frantic efforts by a police officer who saw it happen and the paramedics who were called, the boy died at the scene of the accident. A life full of promise had been cut short on what also happened to be his eighteenth birthday.

Fortunately human tragedies are comparatively rare. The carnage occurs with animals. It is the ponies that capture the headlines because they have come to represent all that is beautiful on Dartmoor together with the heather and the tors but it is sheep and cattle which suffer most and whose deaths often go unreported in the media. Farmers face a tough life with relentless demands on them every day of the year, often at night, and the extra burden placed on them when one of their animals dies or is horribly mutilated in an accident can be devastating.

A graphic example of high-speed driving on the moor. This car cut a Dartmoor pony in two.

Imagine being called from your bed on a winter night because one of your animals is lying dead or injured at the roadside. It might be sleeting with a Dartmoor mist obscuring the area. An injured animal requires the attention of a Vet with the attendant cost to bear and often results in the creature having to be destroyed anyway. The owner is responsible for the cost of having it put down and disposing of the carcass. At the time of writing, in some cases the local hunt will help by sending their own licensed slaughterer to do the job free of charge and if appropriate will dispose of it by feeding the remains to the hounds, a little known feature of the hunting fraternity which many Dartmoor farmers have been grateful for. After perhaps several hours you go back to bed but rise at your usual hour to tend your livestock. You have not only lost a valuable animal which will have to be replaced but if the casualty is a cow or a sheep the individual 'passport' details must be forwarded to the Ministry (registered post only accepted) who must also be notified about the replacement animal. Time and expense and trauma are the extra burdens an owner has to bear when an incident such as this occurs.

A cow may be worth as much as £900 (a sheep £45, a lamb £10, and £50 to £100 for a pony at the time of writing) to which the potential for calf bearing has to be taken into account and in any case death could rob a calf of its mother (the same applies to a lamb or a foal). Those whose animals graze adjacent to the Dousland – Princetown road lose a great many of them each year and the financial burden has become unacceptable. Little wonder they and others have campaigned for this particular road (B3212) and the Tavistock – Princetown road (B3357) to be fenced. The casualty figures are horrendous.

Livestock Deaths on Surveyed Farms.

Figures kindly supplied by Mr. M. Hedges (Dartmoor Society). For each year the numbers include those for two farms whose animals graze adjacent to the B3212 (Dousland – Princetown) and the B3357 Tavistock – Princetown roads. The years 2001/2002 and 2002/2003 refer to those two farms only.

1999/2000		2000/2001		2001/2002		2002/2003	
Sheep	25	Sheep	18	Sheep	24	Sheep	19
Cattle	6	Cattle	3	Cattle	0	Cattle	2
Ponies	11	Ponies	9	Ponies	11	Ponies	11
	42		30		35		32

Temporary signs placed at the roadsides on the moor by Dartmoor National Park Authority, Dartmoor Commoners Council, and Dartmoor Livestock Protection Society during the holiday season.

During ten years motoring to and from Princetown in every kind of weather the author has encountered most types of animal fatalities. He once found two dead lambs with the mother ewe bleating piteously beside them in the middle of the Tavistock – Okehampton road (A386) over Blackdown before that road was fenced (incidentally there has not been an accident involving an animal since). Another time there was a pony with a broken back at Rundlestone with an injured foal in a nearby ditch. Both had to be destroyed. In each case the author was the first to report these incidents (in the latter case a public phone box was just yards away) and the question has to be asked 'What kind of person could inflict such misery and not bother to report it?' Most people agree with the National Park Authority that the majority of accidents are caused by speeding vehicles and the Authority have been trying hard to make drivers aware of this.

A National Park Authority and County Council Perspective

Accidents arise principally where animals roam across the highway. Poor visibility and narrow roads are contributory factors. The Highway Code states: 'Adapt your driving to the appropriate type and conditions of road you are on. Take the road and traffic conditions into account.' Many drivers go too fast and are unable to react quickly enough when animals are on the road.

A Traffic Management Strategy has been developed by Devon County Council, the Highway Authority and the Dartmoor National Park Authority to reduce traffic, lower speeds and improve road safety. A speed limit of 40 mph was introduced over fifty miles of Dartmoor roads in 1995 and extended to cover an additional forty miles in 1996.

People mean food. Ponies are attracted to car parks and roadsides by well meaning but misguided visitors.

Further joint initiatives have included the installation of 'rumble strips', temporary speed indicators, restructuring of roadside verges and trimming vegetation. 'Drive with Moor Care' signs and the use of reflective collars and leg bands for livestock have been supplemented by temporary and permanent information signs, reminders on the back of Ranger Service vehicles and 'Drive With Moor Care' messages in National Park Information Centres and publications. Consequently drivers have been made aware of the hazards and there has been a reduction in animal losses by about 30%.

Whilst livestock losses have fallen, there are still calls for the fencing of roads. Current National Park policies generally presume against fencing on the grounds it would diminish the wild and unspoilt natural beauty that justified Dartmoor's original designation as a National Park. Motor vehicles should not be allowed to dictate changes to the moor and its landscape. The motorist is an impact on the moorland environment and this impact should be minimised rather than imposing works or fencing which would change the character of the moor. Fencing would also impede access by walkers and riders whose crossing points would be restricted. Although a Public Inquiry determined in 1990 that the A386 across Blackdown should be fenced, the Secretary of State indicated that he would be unlikely to support the fencing of further roads in the National Park, stating: 'The A386 is unique among unfenced roads in the National Park in terms of its National Primary status and the volumes of traffic using it'.

Speed limits must not give rise to complacency and a false sense of security, yet there is a very real fear that fencing would lead to even greater complacency and speed. What the limit tells drivers is that the special nature of Dartmoor's roads dictates that 40 mph is a more appropriate maximum speed than 60 mph.

No single measure will resolve the conflict between vehicles, animals and other road users. There are those who ignore warning signs and speed limits (consider the number of motorists who break the 30 mph speed limits in urban areas with the increased risk to human beings including children). The onus will always be on all drivers to drive appropriately to the conditions and potential hazards and it is necessary to sustain driver awareness. In conclusion the National Park Authority and Devon County Council welcome debate and dialogue to help identify solutions to the continuing problem of animal accidents on Dartmoor's roads to ensure that all of us can use these roads safely.

'Ponies were here before cars' the cry is heard but who would say that face to face to the parents of young Andrew Law who will live the rest of their lives lamenting their son? Mr. and Mrs. Law would support any move to prevent such a tragedy happening again.

Drivers and passengers have died in ghastly circumstances. In February 1982 a Ford Cortina car overturned on a bend at Dousland and landed upside down burning furiously. Three teenagers, two of them girls, perished before they could be rescued and the task of recovering their remains left an imprint on the minds of the firemen who attended which will haunt them all their lives. The lone survivor of the crash afterwards said 'I think the driver had taken the corner too fast and over corrected.'

Mr. Cliff Palmer, retired Princetown Fire Brigade Sub Officer, recalls the horror at Merrivale when a cow was struck head on and impaled by a speeding mini, killing beast and driver instantly as it smashed through the windscreen. In another incident in March 1995 a Toyota car hit the retaining wall of Statts Bridge, a short distance from Warren House. Both occupants died, the twisted wreckage of their car bearing testimony to the excessive speed they must have been travelling at (estimated at over 70mph). Yet in certain conditions (ie darkness and thick mist) it is largely a matter of luck whether or not you collide with an animal which happens to wander onto the road (the author was kicked off his motorbike on one occasion by a temperamental mare) and we will never know how many unexplained crashes have occurred as a result of drivers swerving to avoid one. Who can honestly say they have never had a narrow miss?

The subject is highly controversial which is why (it is supposed) two representative parties invited to contribute to this article to lend authority to what is being written, declined to do so. Whilst the hill farmers have sympathy with their associates who constantly lose livestock, some of them feel that fencing of any Dartmoor road would be the 'thin end of the wedge' as they put it. They want their sheep and cattle to roam freely even if they themselves lose an animal or two. As long as hunting remains a legal pursuit its followers also want unrestricted access, as do rambling associations, despite assurances from those who advocate fencing that adequate access points would be provided. A good relationship between ramblers and the farming community is important to both parties; ramblers want to roam and most farmers are happy to let them because many an animal has been saved from dying as a result of walkers reporting their whereabouts and predicament – often with map references to ensure they would be found.

Dartmoor's unique character attracts several million visitors (including local residents) every year – a huge problem in itself. It also supports farming and a host of subsidiary businesses such as guest houses and hotels, restaurants, pubs, cafes and souvenir shops to mention but a few. They all have a fervent (and often conflicting) interest in how Dartmoor should be managed. The Dartmoor National Park Authority tread a tremulous path in their allotted task of preserving all that is best on the moor and at the same time making its peaceful grandeur accessible to everyone. The answer surely is to legislate after consultation with all concerned; to find a way to persuade everyone to try and understand each other's needs and compromise where necessary. The National Park Authority and others are trying to do just this, but maybe even they may have to compromise over certain issues.

Meanwhile the deaths continue, which is why a publication such as this cannot ignore the siuation, and attempts to raise what is hoped are salient points for everyone to consider and possibly act upon.
Footnote: Section 170 of the Road Traffic Act 1988 states:

To comply with a duty under this section to report an accident or to produce such a certificate of insurance or security, or other evidence, as is mentioned in section 165(2)(a) of this Act, the driver-

(a) must do so at a police station or to a constable, and
(b) must do so as soon as is reasonably practicable and, in any case, within twenty-four hours of the occurrence of the accident.

In this section 'animal' means horse, cattle, ass, mule, sheep, pig, goat or dog.

The Policeman's View

After policing Dartmoor's roads for almost twenty years the subject of deaths on the roads is one well known to me. Having attended more animal accidents than I can remember it occurs to me that most of them have involved car drivers who are local and not the visitors. I agree that you cannot always avoid an animal which seems to wait in the darkest place and jump out just as you arrive; but the overwhelming majority of the animal deaths really can be avoided. Speed is the main factor involved followed by the failure to drive carefully past livestock on the open roads. Because there is a 40mph speed limit does not mean that 40mph is always safe, particularly when driving close to grazing roadside sheep. I walk on the moors regularly and never cease to be amazed at the downright recklessness of many car drivers who accelerate past livestock. I am certain that if they had to hold a dying animal still while a Vet destroys it they would think a lot more about the consequences of their inappropriate driving habits. I fear that this is not just a problem for the Dartmoor National Park. The whole thing is about a greater issue of standards of driving and as soon as we raise those standards for every driver then the death toll on our roads will fall – unfortunately it all costs money.

Constable Simon Dell, OBE., QCB.

Acknowledgements.
Dartmoor National Park Authority.
Devon County Council.
P.C. Simon Dell, MBE., QCB.
Mr. and Mrs. R. Law, Princetown.
Mr. Mike Hedges (The Dartmoor Society).
Mr. C. Palmer (Retired long-serving member Princetown Fire Brigade).

ANOTHER LITTLE DRINK (A MISCELLANY).

Visitors to Dartmoor on a sunny day are enthralled with its beauty and tranquillity. When they gaze on the rugged hills and tors, tumbling streams, and all the colourful scenes the place has to offer many of them fail to realise Dartmoor can be a dangerous place for the unwary. The winter months are often Siberian in their ferocity and capable of killing anyone foolhardy enough to venture onto the remote wastes unprepared. Even the military who train there have been known to withdraw their men from the moor because of the severe conditions. The balmy days of summer are not to be taken for granted either. This chapter tells of people who perished on the moor in winter and others who died in mid-summer, all under tragic circumstances.

The author remembers the stark winter of 1947 when exceptional snowstorms swept the area and two people froze to death when their car got stuck overnight in a snowdrift on Roborough Down (no cosy heaters in those days, drivers and passengers wrapped blankets around their knees for comfort). On the high moor later that year the bones of animals – sheep and ponies - were everywhere to be seen and there were pockets of snow lying in some of the hollows as late as June. There have been equally bad winters before and since which sometimes ended in tragedy. In 1792 a skeleton was discovered on the moor which was thought to be that of a sailor who had set out from Plymouth to walk to his home in Chagford. He never arrived. Overtaken by a blizzard he perished and the bones which were found the following spring still had the remnants of his sailor clothes clinging to them.

Many years later another fatality was reported:

The Western Flying Post. Yeovil. Tuesday, January 10th 1865

'A melancholy occurrence took place on Saturday last. A young married man named Sweeney, who had just been appointed as a Schoolteacher to the Dartmoor Convict Prison had gone into Tavistock on business. He left the town on foot to return to Prince Town soon after eight o' clock in the evening.

A heavy snowstorm came on and a fierce wind was blowing at the time, the drifts in some places became many feet deep. Sweeney took over two hours to reach the Merrivale Bridge, a distance of some four miles. There is a public house at the bridge, and here he stopped for a while and partook of refreshment.

The gale had by that time increased in fury, and the landlady urged the poor fellow to stop the night, but being anxious to get home to his wife and young children, he refused the proffered hospitality with thanks, and set out

A Dartmoor River in Flood (Courtesy Paul Rendell)

for his home. He never reached it, his dead body being found the following morning, about three quarters of a mile from Prince Town, in a crouching position close by the hedge'.

Summer days on Dartmoor are often subjected to thunderstorms, some of which are frightening in their magnitude with tremendous downpours. Small streams are transformed into fast swirling torrents in minutes, all of which in turn swell the rivers resulting in white water rapids that come rushing from off the moors in a frightening surge of water with trees, boulders and often the carcasses of drowned sheep or cattle among the debris. When it happens the 'freshets' or 'flash floods' as they are known are preceded by a roaring which can sometimes be heard miles away. The author recalls one such incident in Tavistock many years ago when a rushing wave of water struck Vigo bridge with a shudder and an entire tree, roots and all, became wedged across one of the arches. It was still there weeks later until the water level fell and workmen were available to cut it up and remove it in sections.

As you might expect some unfortunate people have perished in such occurrences. On 17th August 1840 John Edmonds and his wife who had just been married at Staverton Church near Totnes left by horse drawn cart when they were caught in a flood whilst crossing the River Dart and were carried away in a moment. The bride's body was later found wedged in a tree a few hundred yards downstream but the groom was missing for three weeks before his remains were recovered some distance further down. Their horse and cart ended up tumbling over the weir near the bridge at Totnes. The Rev. S. Baring-Gould tells of this event in *A Book of Devon* and goes on to relate how two men approaching Hexworthy on Dartmoor heard the roaring of an approaching flood and ran to cross the wooden bridge they used to cross the river before the it arrived. They were too late. Both men were swept off the bridge and drowned.

Lightning strikes precede the volleys of thunder and they too take their toll on animal and human life. Many a farm hand has been killed after being struck by summer lightning and an event that happened in August 1882 illustrates the point. Farmer William Jackman of Narrator Farm near Sheepstor was haymaking when a thunderstorm began. As the rain pelted down he stuck his pitchfork into a bale of hay and held it over his head as a makeshift 'umbrella' calling to his labourers to do the same. It was his undoing and before they could follow his example a lightning flash struck the metal prongs and was conducted to his body killing him instantly.

In July 1983 Dartmoor Prison Works Dept. employee Cyril Sinclair was inspecting the prison leat between Rundlestone and the headwaters of the River Walkham when a terrific thunderstorm broke. Mr. Sinclair kept in contact with the prison by radio and it was thought lightning may have struck the aerial. When he failed to return or respond to calls a search party was dispatched who found the unfortunate man lying on the footpath by the leat quite dead. A small plain cross on the path marks the spot where this unhappy occurrence took place. This area is notorious for lightning strikes because of its high altitude and exposed location. There have been times when cattle have died on the moor, often in groups - solemn testimony to the intensity of Mother Nature's power.

Accidents with horses were not uncommon on Dartmoor years ago. In August 1863 a twelve year old boy was killed by a runaway horse at Beardown Farm near Two Bridges. He was named in a newspaper report as William Kestle but was in fact William Kistle, a member of the Kistle family who lived at the Ockery outside Princetown. He was returning from Widecombe-in-the-Moor on horseback and had tied the halter to his waist. At the entrance to the farm he somehow fell from the horse which took fright and bolted, dragging young Kistle along the ground for half a mile before being stopped by two men at the farm. Surgeon Askham from Dartmoor Prison attended but there was nothing he could do as the lad was quite dead from a fractured skull.

There were other hazards to contend with in the age of horse and cart

Dartmoor Snow Scene at Two Bridges (Courtesy Paul Rendell)

transport. The steep gradients on Dartmoor hills called for vigilance and a careless moment could cause a fatal accident. This was the case when a Tavistock waggoner lost his life on the summit of Pork Hill on the evening of 1st July 1878. He was thirty three year old John Down who was employed by Tavistock coal merchants Sampson & Son. Having just finished making a delivery in Princetown he was approached by local shoemaker James Willcocks who asked for a lift to Tavistock. They probably knew each other because at Merrivale they halted for a drink at the inn there. Mr. Willcocks testified afterwards that they consumed a quantity of porter before resuming their journey but was adamant that his companion was sober. It was nearing the end of Mr. Down's working day and his thoughts now were of home with his wife and five small children as they made their way up the hill towards the market town and drove along the level at a brisk pace. When they had rounded the bend on the brow of Pork Hill he flicked his whip which startled the horses into a faster pace but with a jerk which unhitched one of the chains connecting the wagon to the shafts. Mr. Down, who was seated at the front of the vehicle with his feet resting on the shafts, leaned over to adjust the loose chain intending to rest his hand for support on the back of one of the two horses pulling them. He missed and fell head first to the ground when the wagon wheels ran over his neck killing him instantly. His horrified passenger jumped from the wagon without stopping the horses and ran back to the unfortunate man but there was nothing he could do for him.

Another distressing event of this kind occurred at a spot near Postbridge in July 1882. Two men from Buckfastleigh took a trip over Dartmoor one weekend, going by train to Totnes on the Saturday where they hired a horse and trap. Woollen factory foreman Richard Gilpin and fellow employee John Marsdon then drove over the moor to Princetown and stayed the night at the Duchy Hotel (now the High Moorland Visitor Centre). On Sunday morning they visited Tavistock and on the return journey stopped for refreshment at the inn at Merrivale. Their trip developed into a drinking spree as they went on to Two Bridges and entered the inn there. Both men were evidently the worse for drink already, so much so the barmaid, after serving then with ale, refused them further drink because she thought they had already consumed enough that day. The pair then decided to go to Postbridge where there was another inn where they could satisfy their wants.

They were soon in trouble. Thomas Rouse noticed them on the road and formed the opinion they were incapable when he saw one of them fall off the trap into the road. Soon afterwards they drove the vehicle into a pond at the side of the road and being unable to free themselves sought help at the Powder Mills (a thriving gunpowder factory at that time). A man called Slee accompanied them and managed to get them back on the road but not before Mr. Marsdon fell into the pond and was immersed. Mr. Slee then took charge and drove the two men to the New Inn (now the East Dart Hotel) at Postbridge where he joined them in a glass of ale and some whisky with water. It was past six o'clock but Marsdon and Gilpin were intent on making the most of their drinking time and had three more glasses of whisky and water. Some time after 9.00pm they left intending to go home via Ashburton.

Around 4.30am on Monday morning Postbridge labourer Thomas Webb was on his way to Princetown where he worked when he came across a man lying beside a trap which was slewed at an angle with one wheel perched on a bank. The horse was quietly grazing nearby. It was obvious the trap had got out of control and pitched at a sufficient slant to have thrown the driver clear. It was John Marsdon and he was dead.

At the Inquest held later at the New Inn Mr. Gilpin said his companion had 'become so intoxicated and obstinate' he decided to leave him with the trap and walked on alone thinking he would follow behind (perhaps they had a disagreement). In fact the dead man was found at a spot some way along the road in the opposite direction to that which he should have taken, an indication perhaps of his confused state of mind. Doctor W.C. Northey who carried out a post-mortem said death was due to 'exposure to night air and damp' (meaning his wet clothes) together with an excess of alcohol which had caused congestion of the brain. This would have affected the unfortunate man's sense of balance. John Marsdon was only thirty two years of age when he died of exposure, alone on the moor on a summer night in July, leaving a poor wife and several children – and all for the sake of 'another little drink'.

The Policeman's View

Over twenty years of policing the Dartmoor area and a similar time as a member of the Dartmoor Rescue Group has proved to me that Dartmoor does not take kindly to those who fail to treat it with the dignity and respect it deserves. Even those who adopt all the sensible precautions that might reasonably be taken can find themselves at its mercy when the weather suddenly changes for the worse or illness overtakes the luckless walker. I well recall a glorious sunny afternoon in April 1981. I had walked in shirtsleeves to assist in rescuing an unfortunate police cadet with a broken leg in the Plym valley. Within twenty four hours I was snowed-in, sleeping on the floor at Princetown Police Station for two days during a long rescue to recover some ATC cadets lost in blizzards.

Alcohol and sheer stupidity has often been the catalyst for disaster on the moors but equally Dartmoor's sheer beauty and remoteness has attracted those poor souls who wish to end their days amid its tranquillity. Whenever I have ventured far out to recover such an individual I have often taken a moment to sit and reflect upon what would have been their last view of this mortal world of ours. I have always come away humbled in the knowledge that whilst Dartmoor can be unforgiving and sometimes unmerciful, it is also a place whose beauty and magnificence is rarely equalled anywhere. If I were to choose a view to gaze upon when my 'time' comes I could think of none better.

Constable Simon Dell, MBE., QCB.

Acknowledgements.
Constable Simon Dell MBE., QCB.
Mr. David Worth, Princetown.
A Book of Devon by Rev. S. Baring-Gould.
Tavistock Gazette.

MURDER ON VALENTINE'S DAY.

When John Maxwell* took his wife for a drive one evening it was allegedly to discuss a reconciliation (the Maxwells had separated after eight years of marriage and had lived apart for several years). The husband had other plans though and drove his wife to a lonely stretch of road on the edge of Dartmoor where he stopped and killed her in a most brutal manner before driving over her to make it look as if there had been a tragic road accident. It was 14th February 1959 – Valentine's Day and he almost got away with it.

This chapter relates how an alert country 'Bobby' only eleven months out of his probationary service foiled a murderer's cover story by alerting his CID colleagues to a minor circumstance he felt uneasy about. His action brought a killer to justice and earned a Commendation for all those involved.

At 7.40pm that fateful day a Dousland resident and his wife were driving along the Walkhampton – Horrabridge road when they were confronted by a woman's body lying in the road and a short distance beyond was a stationary vehicle on the offside. Maxwell was waving a torch to alert them and asked for help. It was his wife he said, she had fallen from his car and the rear wheel had gone over her – could they summon an ambulance or a doctor? They continued their journey to Horrabridge and phoned the police.

First to arrive were two policemen based at Yelverton one of whom was twenty three year old Constable Brian Phillips. He had summoned an ambulance and a doctor who on arrival pronounced the woman dead. Her husband told him he had been negotiating a bend in the road when his wife dropped some articles from her handbag and in trying to retrieve them she must have disturbed the door handle causing the door to open and precipitating her out of the car. He had braked hard and stopped on the offside a short distance in front of his wife's body – his vehicle apparently always veered to the right when the brakes were applied.

A description of the vehicle will enable the reader to appreciate the circumstances surrounding this incident. It was what was called a 'shooting brake' the forerunner of the estate car. The bodywork was constructed mainly of wood and the car was in fact a converted jeep with a left hand drive. It should be noted the doors opened backwards and there was a mere nine inches (approx. twenty three centimetres) between the bottom edges and the ground. There were many such vehicles around at that time and most of

* John Maxwell is a pseudonym to protect surviving family members.

them would not be allowed on the roads today. There were no M.O.T. tests in those days and no seatbelts. Mr. Maxwell's car was in a dilapidated condition and he actually used this fact to partially explain the cause of the accident! It was also a contributory factor in convicting him.

After the body had been removed Constable Phillips decided to accompany Mr. Maxwell to his sister-in-law's house in Horrabridge where he was to spend the night. The first thing Maxwell did was reach across and fasten a bolt on the passenger door. When asked about the accident and whether the bolt was in place when his wife was seated there he said he had forgotten to fasten it. During the journey and despite it being a dark winter night the Constable noticed a number of minute spots on the interior of the windscreen. His curiosity aroused he took a closer look with the aid of his torch and found them to be flecks of blood. Maxwell confirmed this saying he had taken a cloth from above the screen to support his wife's head and that he had blood on his hands from her body (she had severe head injuries and was covered in blood) which must have dripped inside the car. By now the young policeman was 'uneasy' as he later put it during a telephone call to a CID colleague who asked if he was satisfied the event had been a straightforward road accident. Consequently, after Maxwell had received a sedative from the doctor and been advised to go to bed, Constable Phillips and the doctor were joined by Police Sergeant Lee at the Horrabridge address and together they examined the interior of the car.

Police Officer Phillips (Courtesy B. Phillips)

More bloodstains were discovered together with smears of blood which had run down the woodwork below the passenger door window. To their surprise Maxwell then appeared carrying a glass container and he in turn seemed surprised to see them (the car was parked in the road fifty feet from

COMMENDATION

DETECTIVE SERGEANT 166 TARR, C.J. (Officer in charge of Enquiry).
DETECTIVE CONSTABLE 399 HARPER, D.R.A. (Photographer).
CONSTABLE 624 HURN, F.J. (Preparation of Plan).
M.P. CONSTABLE 295 BURGESS, J.E.J. (Examination of Vehicle).
SERGEANT 478 LEE, R.A.
CONSTABLE 308 PHILLIPS, B.J.

     The above officers were all concerned in the investigations into the death of Mrs.   on February 14th 1959. At the time of her death she was accompanied in her husband's car by her husband,   who was suspected of having attacked her in the car, bludgeoned her there, and later on the neighbouring moor, and finally run over her with his car on the road in order to simulate death as a result of a road accident. The investigation was a very comprehensive one involving a great deal of circumstantial evidence, and the Police Officers from the start exhibited remarkable attention to detail.

                was convicted of murder at the Devon Summer Assize on June 19th and sentenced to life imprisonment. The Trial Judge, Mr. Justice Donovan stated in Court that Detective Sergeant Tarr and his other officers engaged should be commended upon their efforts. The Director of Public Prosecutions has made the following remarks in an official letter –

     "This case has provided an outstanding example of the value of meticulous attention to detail in the investigation of crime. In particular, I feel that special mention should be made of Police Constable PHILLIPS whose powers of observation when originally called to the scene ensured that the case was treated as one of suspected murder within a very short time of its commission. But the case was excellently handled throughout and reflects very great credit upon all the officers concerned."

     This has been one of the best performed enquiries in the annals of the Devon Constabulary, and reflects great credit on the Police Work of the Force as a whole. I have great pleasure in awarding commendations to all the officers named.

               (Signed) R.M.Bacon.

                  Lieut. Colonel.

               Chief Constable of Devon.

The Commendation from the Chief Constable

the house). His excuse was he had come outside to get some paraffin for lighting the fire in the morning (a common practice at that time when fires were doused overnight and re-lit next day) but had he intended using the paraffin to remove the bloodstains? Both officers decided there were sufficient grounds for further investigation and they went to where the incident occurred to examine the road by torchlight. What they found led them to believe all was not as Mr. Maxwell had described. PC Phillips had previously marked with chalk the positions where the body and car were when he first arrived. There were bloodstains and fresh oil drips on the road where the car had been. Further examination revealed blood and oil on the road at a point further back from where the body had lain which suggested the car had stopped there previous to her death. It was decided to come back in daylight and carry out a thorough search of the area.

CID officers now took over the investigation and what they found next day turned suspicions into near certainty. The mortuary had been instructed to leave Mrs. Maxwell's body clothed and undisturbed in order for a Pathologist to carry out a post mortem examination. Dr. Stewart Smith the Pathologist for the Exeter area examined the body and visited the scene of the tragedy. He concluded death was due to multiple injuries to the head. He found a depression in the wife's head consistent with being run over by the wheel of a car but there were a number of smaller injuries to the head of sufficient force to fracture the skull. These were in his opinion inflicted by a blunt instrument and a toolbox behind the driver's seat and easily accessible to him was found to contain hammers one of which had traces of blood on the handle. More significantly were smudges of clay and particles of shale adhering to the dead woman's clothing which could not have been picked up from the tarmac road. The torso did not sustain abrasive injuries of the type normally associated with someone coming into contact with a tarmac road. These revelations tied in neatly with discoveries made on site when detectives came across a two feet wide swathe of disturbed material, mainly clay and shale, some distance back from where the body was. The indications were that Mrs. Maxwell had somehow been propelled across a grass verge and down a rough bank leading to common ground and had been dragged feet first up the bank and laid in the road. Then bloodstained stones were discovered at various distances from the bottom of the bank; a knitted glove lay nearby (which matched the one glove found on the body) and a small thorn bush with splashes of blood on it (this bush was taken up and later exhibited in court together with the stones). It was now apparent the police

The murder scene

had a murder to deal with but how were they to build a concrete case against Maxwell?

No effort was spared to gather irrefutable evidence for the prosecution. Motor Patrol Constable J. Burgess examined the car and tested the brakes: the car veered to the left not to the right as Maxwell claimed. A practical test by a lady assistant groping on the floor of the car to retrieve some articles failed to operate the passenger door handle by bodily movement and the door stayed firmly shut even after heavy pressure was applied against it. A layer of undisturbed mud adhering to the underside of the chassis led to the conclusion a body had not been dragged beneath the car and run over by the rear wheel as the accused claimed (in any case the aforementioned nine inch clearance would not have permitted it). Attention now focussed on the oil spots found on the road several of which had a distinctive 'L' shape. The poorly maintained vehicle had a profuse oil leak from the engine which ran down the casing leaving just such an oil stain. It was as good as a fingerprint and such a mark could not have been left if the car had been moving. The vehicle itself was providing evidence against its owner.

Under questioning Maxwell could not account for any of the anomalies and had no explanation to offer, sticking to his original story. He was subsequently charged with murder. The police interpreted the sequence of events as follows.

For some reason Maxwell had stopped the car where the first oil stains marked the road and attacked his wife in the passenger seat, probably with a hammer from the toolbox. Mrs. Maxwell managed to get out and ran for her life down the bank pursued by her husband. Around the area of the thorn bush he battered her again with the bloodstained stones which were found scattered nearby and dragged her up the bank onto the road where he reversed the rear wheel over her head (there was blood on the rear tyre of the car) This accounted for the large depression in her skull noted by the pathologist and the clay soil and shale fragments found adhering to her clothing. He then parked his vehicle on the offside of the road a little further along to give the impression his wife had fallen out and landed where she was lying.

Home Office Pathologist Dr. C.A. Hunt and an assistant were now called to examine the vehicle and the ground where the incident occurred. They were able to show all bloodstains in the road, in the area around the thorn bush, on the bush and the stones as well as in the vehicle were all of type 'B' the same as that of the dead woman. Furthermore several strands of human hair were found adhering to the car door, rear tyre, the thorn bush and several stones nearby as well as fibres from the dead woman's clothing. There was no blood or hair found under the vehicle consistent with an accidental fall from it. Meanwhile the suspect's clothing was taken for examination during the course of which further incriminating evidence came to light. His shoes were sparkling clean when taken possession of and he had washed the overalls he had worn and left them drying over the fire. All the same bloodstains were detected on other items of clothing and his shoes had traces of blood, clay and shale embedded in the soles.

To clinch the prosecution case Det. Sergeant C.J. Tarr who led the investigation drove at 30 mph along the two routes Maxwell could have taken from Lutton (where he had called with his wife in the car to collect some belongings from his sister's house and left just before 7.00pm) to the murder scene. Either way it left the accused an uninterrupted half an hour to commit the murder and stage the 'accident' until the car came along.

The defence, led by Mr. N. Skelhorn QC at the June sitting of Devon Assizes, faced a formidable task as no convincing argument could be made in the light of Maxwell's previous statements. Mr. J.T. Moloney, for the prosecution hammered home the main points outlined above and despite a spirited defence the jury took a mere forty minutes to return a 'Guilty' verdict. After sentencing Maxwell to life imprisonment Mr. Justice Donovan recommended that all the police officers engaged in this case should be

The vehicle

commended for their efforts. This was subsequently done and in an official letter the Director of Public Prosecutions said: 'This case has provided an outstanding example of the value of meticulous attention to detail in the investigation of crime. In particular, I feel that special mention should be made of Police Constable Phillips whose powers of observation when originally called to the scene ensured that the case was treated as one of suspected murder within a very short time of its commission. But the case was excellently handled throughout and reflects very great credit on all the officers concerned'.

A delighted Chief Constable of Devon, Lieut. Colonel R.M. Bacon, commented: 'This has been one of the best performed enquiries in the annals of the Devon Constabulary and reflects great credit on the Police Work of the Force as a whole. I have great pleasure in awarding commendations to all the officers named'. They were: Detective Sergeant C.J. Tarr (who took charge of the enquiry). Detective Constable D.R.A. Harper (photographer). Constable F.J. Hurn (who drew a first class plan of the scene). Motor Patrol Constable J.E.J. Burgess (who examined the vehicle). Sergeant R.A. Lee from Tavistock (who detected the singular oil stains). Constable B.J. Phillips – (the young inexperienced police officer who rose to become Assistant Chief Constable of Devon and Cornwall Constabulary).

The Policeman's View.

Being the first police officer at the scene of any death you have a great weight of responsibility placed upon you to ensure that no foul play has occurred. You have no team of detectives or scientists at your side in those first few crucial minutes. Your initial 'gut feeling' based on the facts as you see them is all you have to work on. Constable Phillips could well have missed the small blood spots in the dark or have been taken-in by the offender's explanation. Instead his policeman's intuition made him look closer. Had he not done so this whole matter would have been recorded as a tragic road accident and a guilty man would have walked free. Here I am with only a few years to go before retirement from the Force (I was only a few months old at the time of this murder) but I knew many of the officers involved in this investigation as they themselves approached their own final years of service. I regarded all of them as role models for my own future in the Force. Jack Tarr went on to become head of the CID in Devon & Cornwall and John Hurn later became a Scenes of Crime Officer. I know that Brian Phillips dismisses any accolade, insisting that the success of the investigation relied upon team-work, but that team-work only came about through a young constable's keen eye to attention and detail so richly deserving of the commendations awarded to them all.

Constable Simon Dell, MBE., QCB.

Acknowledgments.
Assistant Chief Constable (Rtd.) Brian Phillips QPM
Constable Simon Dell, MBE., QCB.
Western Morning News.
Sunday Independent.
Tavistock Times.
Tavistock Gazette.
Express and Echo (Exeter).
Western Times.

DEADMANS BOTTOM

A 'bottom' on Dartmoor is a shallow valley which branches off from a larger one and is usually closed at its upper end. There are many 'bottoms' on the moor and all of them have names. 'Deadmans Bottom' relates to an incident long ago when the body of a man was discovered there. Tradition has it that the Parish in which it then was did not want the responsibility of burying him and this task was taken up by the neighbouring Parish who promptly laid claim to that part of the moor. It now lies within the boundaries of that Parish.

Countless people have got lost on Dartmoor and had to be rescued, some of them in the nick of time having been exposed to the worst of weather and suffering from weakness and hypothermia. The Dartmoor Rescue Group (the first group was formed at Tavistock in 1968) maintain a proud and successful record in this respect, often turning out at a moment's notice in atrocious weather in answer to an emergency call - and every man a volunteer. Many a lost or injured walker, some of them very young, have had cause to bless them as they were escorted or carried off the moor cold, wet and exhausted - but safe at last.

George Turner did not come into this category because he knew exactly where he was going and how to get there and back which is why his family quickly became concerned when he failed to return at his estimated time. He was an ex-Colour Sergeant in the Royal Marines with twenty one years service and knew Dartmoor well having done a large part of his commando training there. He had been an active man all his life and had an abiding love of the moor. At sixty years of age and after undergoing a heart by-pass operation he continued regular Saturday excursions, weather permitting. He would pack his rucksack and set off from his home at Woodford in Plymouth for Cadover Bridge, his usual starting point for a circular walk that would finish by early evening, leaving his wife a list of his intended destinations to allay any worries she might have and because he was by nature a methodical man. His check list included not only his destinations but map references and compass bearings too plus the estimated times he reckoned it would take him to walk the routes he knew so well.

On Saturday 18th June 1988 he left home for a hike on the moor after telling Mrs. Turner to expect him back at around 4.00pm and as usual gave her a list of places he would be heading for with the relevant details. Four o'clock came and preparations were under way at home pending his return, but the minutes and hours went by without any homecoming and by 6.00pm the family were so concerned his son-in-law Mr. Ray Wills went to Cadover and found Mr. Turner's car exactly as he had left it. It had been a beautiful day, sunny and warm and there had been no reason to suppose he would be delayed by bad weather - a Dartmoor mist for example. Understandably therefore the family became alarmed and the police were notified. Officers with tracker dogs went to Dartmoor and began a wide-ranging search with the help of a police helicopter and sections of the Dartmoor Rescue Group from Plymouth and Tavistock. Neighbours of the Turner family (Messrs. Jeff Yates, Gerald Lapthorn and David Long) joined the hunt for their friend all through

Colour Sgt. George Turner, Royal Marines (Courtesy Mrs. B. Turner)

the night and into Sunday by which time all the searchers were extremely tired and frustrated. Every location George Turner indicated he would visit en route had been investigated together with the adjacent areas but without result. The weather continued fine and sunny on Sunday with good visibility yet no sign of the missing man could be found – an indication of just how remote and wide some areas of Dartmoor are. Where was he? Was he lying injured or been taken ill somewhere hidden from view? These questions inevitably arose as the hours went by.

During Sunday the weary rescue teams from Tavistock and Plymouth were stood down and sent home to get some sleep and something to eat, expecting to be recalled that night if necessary. They were relieved by Dartmoor Rescue Group from Ashburton and Okehampton. By evening, when the searchers had still not found him, it became apparent it must be a body they were looking for but where? Tavistock Community Policeman Simon Dell, who was a member of the Tavistock Dartmoor Rescue Group

Deadmans Bottom (Courtesy Paul Rendell)

and who had assisted non-stop for almost twenty four hours, now assumed control in his new capacity of Investigation Officer. He realised there were two potential flaws if they continued working as they had done. Firstly the ground had been criss-crossed by so many individuals, each of whom had left a 'scent', and the tracker dogs were clearly confused. The second consideration was made apparent later and proved to be a lesson to take note of for future operations of this kind. The search teams had been directed to various locations on Mr. Turner's route and scoured the surrounding areas but what had not occurred to anyone was the fact that there were different routes he might have taken to get from one landmark to another and this could be the key to finding him. P.C. Dell managed to persuade all those involved to vacate the moor overnight with the intention of resuming the search early Monday morning with a limited number of dog-handlers, by which time all traces of human scent would have dissipated and the air-scent dogs of the Dartmoor Rescue Group would have a chance of following a single positive scent.

Early Monday morning, accompanied by Clive Turner and Graham Lobb (the missing man's son and nephew respectively) he returned to the moor by Land Rover and set up a control point at Eylesbarrow Mine which afforded a panoramic view of the search area. Before commencing the planned operations however another Land Rover appeared with Chief Inspector Tony Booth of the R.S.P.C.A accompanied by Dartmoor National Park Ranger Paul Salmon. They were looking for an injured pony which a member of the public had reported but were only too willing to assist in the hunt for Mr. Turner as well. Knowing that Chief Inspector Booth was an experienced Dartmoor walker, P.C. Dell asked him what route he would take to walk from their location to another landmark some distance away which was mentioned on the missing man's check list. The Chief Inspector was in no doubt which way he would go and set off with the Ranger in that direction promising to report anything suspicious they might see. It was to be the breakthrough P.C. Dell was looking for.

As they drove across the ridge overlooking marshes and combes below Little Gnats Head they saw a body – it was George Turner lying face down in Deadmans Bottom. Mobile phones were not available at that time and it took three radio calls to inform P.C. Dell of their find, first to the R.S.P.C.A. Headquarters in Exeter who in turn contacted police in Plymouth who then radioed their man at Eyelesbarrow. A policeman's instinct had paid off and events now proceeded in a set pattern: no-one was to disturb or go near the body until a routine examination by the police officer was carried out. Because of the remote location and clear evidence of death a doctor was not summoned to pronounce the man dead, this was to be done later at the hospital. Mr.Turner's son Clive had the distressing task of identifying his father.

The final task was to arrange for the body to be transported off the moor and here fate took a hand in a way that brought some comfort to the bereaved. A Royal Navy helicopter was seen hovering some distance away which prompted P C Dell to radio their base at Coypool (Plymouth) to enquire if it was possible for them to help. Yes it was – there was a lull during the exercise they were engaged in and consequently the aircraft was sent and guided to the spot by P C Dell letting off flares. Imagine the surprise on the faces of all concerned when two Royal Marines emerged from it (the helicopter was manned exclusively by Royal Marines) and Colour Sergeant

FROM	TO	GRID REF	BEARING	TIME
555 646	JUNCTION			
CADOVER BRIDGE	PLYM & BLACKA BROOK	564 644	102+6 = 105°	12+
JUNCTION PLYM & BLACKA BROOK	STONE ROWS	576 638	112+6 = 115°	15+
" STONE ROWS	BS	591 632	116+6 = 122	18+
BS	TRIG POINT BS	603 645	40+6 = 46	24+
TRIG POINT BS	LANGCOMBE HILL MOUND & BS	615 655	52+6 = 58°	30+
LANGCOMBE MOUND & BS	NR LANGCOMBE HEAD	620 663	32+6 = 38 5°	24+
NR LANGCOMBE HEAD	RETURN BY LANGCOMBE BROOK & PLYM. JUNCTION	602 673	298+6 = 304°	
To extend above.				123+
Mound & BS NR LANGOMB HEAD	ERME PITS	624 668	25+6 = 31°	9+
ERME PITS	DRY LAKE FORD	635 664	110+6 = 116°	15+
DRY LAKE FORD	RED LAKE FORD	643 664	85+6 = 91°	9+
RED LAKE FORD	CROSS WAYS	650 658	126+6 = 132	12+
CROSS WAYS	RED LAKE CHINA CLAY WORKS	646 670	342+6 = 348	15+
GREEN HILL ——→		635 678	310+6 = 316°	15+
GREEN HILL	POST	631 681	296+6 = 304	9+
POST	PLY HEAD.	622 684	284+6 = 290°	15+
RETURN BY PLYM				102

Example of the route plans Mr Turner always gave his wife. (Courtesy Mrs B. Turner)

George Turner was gently taken up and put on board. Never was a man carried in such a respectful manner Simon Dell later recalled. He accompanied the body to a rendezvous at Cox Tor car park where the Royal Marines crew again bore the body to a waiting hearse.

An Inquest recorded a verdict of 'Heart Failure'. Mr. Turner was cremated and his ashes scattered on Brentor, a favourite spot for him and his family. The little church on the tor needed a new Communion Cup and the family considered it appropriate to provide one dedicated to his memory and this they did. Fifteen years later a brave Mrs. Turner discussed these events with the author who asked: 'What would her husband have said if he had known he would be found in Deadmans Bottom?' Her face lit up and the reply was instantaneous: 'Oh, he would have thought it a huge joke and had a good laugh' she said.

The Policeman's View

After more than twenty seven years of being a policeman I have dealt with countless sudden deaths, many long forgotten to me, but each one still a cherished memory to a loved one left behind. How can one policeman remember every single incident for over a quarter of a century? However, there are some which are indelibly printed on my mind and none more so than my involvement with the late George Turner. I never knew him in life, I wish I did. I have found out so much about him since the events of that summer day that I am envious of those whose lives he touched and a walk along the Plym valley always brings memories of that weekend back to me.

George had left a meticulous route plan of his journey just in case, and he was found exactly on his route. As I go for my frequent walks on the moors I often think that when eventually 'my time comes' I hope and pray that I will be as blessed as George. From spending time piecing together his last few hours I know that he died looking at the most glorious morning view of the moors ahead as he walked eastwards, feeling in the best of health and enjoying a passion for the moors shared by us both. I am confident in making such assertions because of the evidence which George left us; fate has ensured that we know that all was well with him at the end.

I found him lying on his front, his hands beside him, head to the east. I will always remember that his green woollen service shirt had its top button done up and the chest strap on his ruck-sack was also tightly secured. You might wonder how this tells us so much. To me I saw the body of a clearly fit man who had died without putting his hands out instinctively to break his fall. No man hits the ground with his hands beside him, unless he is dead or deeply unconscious. I am sure he died before he struck the ground. His head was to the east on his outward journey so he died in the morning looking along the valley of the Plym. The morning was glorious, skylarks filled the air and the warmth of the sun was upon him. If he had been feeling unwell he would have stopped, he would have sat down and perhaps collapsed from a sitting position. He would have unbuttoned his top button and at least loosened his ruck-sack. He had done none of these things. He had left this life with expedience and dignity, on a true course and in the company and presence of his creator. His final journey from his beloved moor was borne by Her Majesty's Royal Marines whose solemnity and respect was a credit to them and to him. All that was lacking were the words to my favourite Psalm - "I will lift up mine eyes unto the hills." But I added them some years later for him at - 'Dead Mans Bottom'.

Constable Simon Dell, OBE., QCB.

Acknowledgements.
Mrs. B. Turner, widow.
P.C. Simon Dell, OBE., QCB.
Crossings Guide to Dartmoor by William Crossing.

ALONE ON THE MOOR.

Dartmoor keeps its secrets well. Huge areas of the moor were rarely visited seventy or more years ago and even today it is possible to find complete solitude there if one desires it. Yet the most puzzling mysteries of all have occurred within a couple of miles or so as the crow flies from the main road at Postbridge and close to farms and houses. In this area two men, both strangers to the moor, perished alone and a long way from home yet so near to the help that might have saved them. The circumstances surrounding these events have never been satisfactorily explained.

Readers will recall the strange story of Walton Howard where a body was found in November 1934 on the slopes of Row Tor above Archerton in circumstances which were never fully explained. Another baffling affair took place twenty years previously in which there were a number of remarkable similarities.

The month of February 1914 had been largely wet and windy on the moor but Saturday 21st brought better weather which prompted Mr. George French of Hartland Farm near Postbridge to go rabbiting with his brother-in-law. It was during one of their successful chases in one of his own newtakes that Mr. French stumbled upon the body of a man hidden under some furze bushes and lying face down on a waterproof sheet. It was evident the body had been there several days.

P.C. Weekes the Princetown policeman was sent for. After examining the body and searching the dead man's clothing the corpse was carried with great difficulty over rough ground to a waiting vehicle and taken to Princetown mortuary prior to a post-mortem and inquest. The man was estimated to be thirty five years old, was clean shaven, about six feet tall with long black hair, blue eyes, and of slight build. He was well dressed in a heavy dark overcoat, grey jacket, a blue tie with white spots, waistcoat, brown breeches with matching stockings and black boots. It was apparent he had planned to be travelling for several days as he had shaving kit in one of his pockets as well as £20 in gold inside a purse on a chain, some loose change, and a Dartmoor guide book. He did not have a stick, a map, food and drink, or a bag. Altogether he represented a respectable type of man not suited to long hikes over Dartmoor. The similarities with the Walton Howard case are at once noticeable – found alone in odd circumstances, well dressed (even wearing a spotted tie!) young, tall, and not carrying any means of identification. There was more to come. A further search of the man's clothing

William Donaghy Memorial Stone at Hartland Tor   (Author's photo)

by P.C. Weekes after arriving at Princetown (it was then 8.00pm) revealed a scrap of paper torn from the guide book on which was written: 'W. Donaghy, Aigburth, Liverpool' and 'J. Donaghy, Roulyn Street, St. Michaels, Liverpool'. Telephone enquiries to Liverpool police resulted in Mr. James Donaghy, a cashier with the Midland Railway at Liverpool, coming forward to reveal he was the dead man's brother and identifying him as thirty one year old William Donaghy of Aigburn, Liverpool, who had disappeared in November 1913 (Walton Howard was also thirty one). He was the Science Master at Warrington Technical School, which was not only situated in Walton Howard's home town but was the Institute he attended to obtain the qualifications for his job as Foreman in a tannery. He had given no indication about where he was going (neither did Walton H.) and after drawing a substantial sum (£50) from his bank account (just like Walton H.) he vanished. Unlike Walton however he did send a letter to his brother which stated: 'Dear Jim, please settle my affairs as best you can. I am going away'.

Mr. Donaghy also said his brother had an internal complaint which could cause morbid melancholia but thought it unlikely he would do anything rash (there was no sign of a struggle or self harm when the body was found) and intimated if he did contemplate suicide he had access to several deadly poisons at the Technical School where he worked. Every effort was made to trace the missing man by enquiries and newspaper adverts but it was of no avail – even his fiancée heard nothing from him.

The Princetown policeman made another discovery when searching the dead man's clothes: a railway cloakroom ticket dated 4th February at the Queen Street (Exeter) railway station. An investigation there revealed he had assumed an alias (Jones) and uncovered a bag containing personal effects including a knife; a watch and chain; and a revolver with nineteen live rounds. A number of questions inevitably arose: Where on earth did he obtain a revolver and ammunition? Was it his intention to retrieve it and use it to end his life? Why did he leave his belongings at the station? Where was he heading for on the moor? Did he have a mental breakdown and simply wander off the road only to be caught in a sudden rainstorm and seek shelter under the furze where he was found?

On Tuesday 24th February an Inquest was held at Princetown. James Donaghy gave his evidence as outlined above, adding that a medical advisor was of the opinion his brother would have gone to some quiet place where he would be free of worry. His physical condition had been brought about by 'excessive exertion' (another term for overwork or stress perhaps?) Dr. C. Brodrick of Tavistock who performed a post-mortem examination on the deceased stated that apart from a thin body all the internal organs were healthy and that death was caused by syncope (loss of consciousness due to low blood pressure) following exposure. As this was consistent with the known facts and winter conditions on Dartmoor the Jury returned a verdict in accordance with Dr. Brodrick's report.

As with the Walton Howard case William Donaghy was taken home for burial. Some time afterwards a memorial for him appeared on the face of a large boulder. The inscription reads:

IN MEMORY OF
WILLIAM DONAGHY
OF LIVERPOOL WHO DIED BESIDE THIS STONE
FEBRUARY 1914

This prompts the question: who provided the memorial? Furthermore there was no mention of a stone in the account given by Mr. French about the discovery of the body - just the furze bush was alluded to. Perhaps the stone lies near the spot where William Donaghy perished; it is a strange legacy pertaining to an even stranger event. Walton Howard has no memorial on Dartmoor.

LOST SOLDIERS ON THE MOOR.

It has been said the British Army first came to Dartmoor in the 1870s to camp on the moor and carry out manoeuvres. In fact soldiers were on the moor during the Napoleonic Wars (1803–1815) to man the Prisoner of War Depot at Princetown. The army resumed this role in November 1850 when the First Battalion of the King's Own Royal Regiment (4th. of Foot) arrived to guard the prisoners at the newly opened Dartmoor Convict Prison. They were responsible for the security of the convicts whenever they were out of their cell blocks for church parades and work parties etc. Various other army units in turn succeeded them until April 1854 when the Civil Guard was formed.

The terrible winters of that era are a rare event now and one can scarcely comprehend the intensity of cold and suffering endured by prisoners and sentries alike. This is a story of endurance which ended in tragedy and generated a legend.

The winter of 1853 was a severe one on Dartmoor. The rugged splendour of the moor was hidden beneath undulating snow drifts several foot deep which lent the place a benign appearance and an attractive one. For the convicts and their guardians at the prison however the snow brought great hardship when the prison leat froze over and every road to Princetown became impassable. The result was an acute shortage of water and food and the convicts had to make do on half rations whilst the soldiers were reduced to scrounging flour from the Duchy Hotel with which they made a little dough to bake on shovels over open fires. The garrison now comprised a Company of the 7th. Regiment Royal Fusiliers whose name is derived from the word 'Fusil' an early type of musket – so they were infantrymen, the toughest of troops.

On Saturday 12th February two Fusiliers, Privates George Driver and Patrick Carlin, who had recently been discharged from the Royal Military Hospital at Devonport, were at their headquarters in St. Georges Square waiting to be escorted back to their barracks at Princetown. A Corporal Ramsden went with them for the first seven miles to the village of Jump (now Roborough) where they were handed over to Corporal John Penton who had tramped from Princetown to collect them for the final ten miles of their journey. It had been snowing heavily and the trip from Dartmoor to Jump had been an epic in itself. The Corporal was accompanied by John Smith of No. 3 Company (who was returning to Devonport) and it took them four hours to get as far as Dousland, a distance of five miles, floundering up to their armpits at times among the drifts They must have been numbed and soaking wet by the time

A wintery scene leading to Princetown (Courtesy Paul Rendell)

they met up with the Devonport party and Smith did all he could to dissuade Penton from attempting to cross the moor a second time that day but to no avail. 'Duty is duty' was Penton's remark as the three Fusiliers trudged away. They stopped for a short while at the Dousland Barn Inn where the landlord strongly advised them not to attempt the rest of their trip but again Corporal Penton insisted 'orders are orders' as they resumed their journey. They were not seen alive again.

It was afterwards concluded by the search parties who went looking for them they must have encountered the deep snow drift they found at the summit of Peek Hill on the edge of the moor, but were able to get clear of it and get as far as Devils Bridge where another drift prevented further progress. Lost or discarded caps and knapsacks marked their trail. The two Privates evidently made it back to the first drift where they must have perished from cold and exhaustion, their bodies being discovered the next day (Sunday). But where was Penton? It took until Monday to find him at a spot known as Soldiers Pond just off the road and only 200 yards from the Duchy Hotel; he had obviously made a determined effort to press on alone for help and very nearly succeeded. He was only twenty years of age and recently married.

Conditions on the moor must have eased considerably for the Inquest to be held at the barracks in Princetown on Friday 18th February where a verdict of 'Accidental Death' was recorded. The three men were buried on Sunday 20th February with full military honours and it was a significant event with spectators coming from miles around to pay their respects. The

'Three Valiant Soldiers' as they came to be called lie together in a communal grave in the churchyard of St. Michaels and All Angels, the Parish Church in Princetown. The grave is situated at the rear of the church behind the tower and adjacent to the churchyard boundary wall. It has a slate Memorial.

IN MEMORY OF
Three Valiant Soldiers
of the 7th Royal Fusiliers
who died on Dartmoor
in a snowdrift 12th Feb 1853
Corp Joseph Penton Aged 20
Private Patrick Carlin Aged 23
Geo. Driver Aged 27

(Photo courtesy Paul Rendell)

The Policeman's View

I can't help but wonder if Walton Howard knew of the circumstances of the death of William Donaghy. The similarities are great. Equally, when the death of Walton Howard was being investigated were the strange circumstances which took place twenty years previously also looked into as possibly being connected? If such a death occurred now both incidents would be closely scrutinised for similarities and possible connections. I find the similarities between Howard's death and the one which took place at Beachy Head such that this was no mere coincidence; and equally the uncanny similarities between Howard and Donaghy's deaths are too much to just ignore – even if twenty years had elapsed. Unfortunately Dartmoor has decided to keep the secret for itself and I know of no greater 'keeper of confidences' than the moor.

The sad story of the Valiant Soldiers tells us much about not only military discipline but perhaps more about nineteenth century discipline and state of mind. It is hard to imagine these days well-trained soldiers losing their lives on the open moors but I sit and write this less than a week after thirty five military recruits managed to get themselves lost on the moors necessitating the Police being called to organise a search party for them. Fortunately they found their way to safety but perhaps both events, over a century apart, are proof that nobody must ever take the moors for granted and that Dartmoor will always choose its own moment to punish those who do not respect how harsh it can be.

Constable Simon Dell, MBE., QCB.

Acknowledgements.

William Donaghy:

Western Morning News	(23 Feb. 1914).
Western Evening Herald	(24 Feb. 1914).
Western Daily Mercury	(28 Feb. 1914).

Dartmoor Newsletter article by Adrienne Yelland May 1993.

Three Valiant Soldiers:

Mr. David Worth, Princetown.
Plymouth Times, Devonport, Stonehouse and West of England Advertiser (two issues in Feb. 1853).

MASS GRAVES AND OTHER PRISON EVENTS.

At the rear of Dartmoor prison, outside the boundary walls and sheltered by trees, are two mass graves where the remains of more than 1500 prisoners of war are interred. The prison was constructed to hold French prisoners taken during the Napoleonic Wars and the first of them came to Dartmoor in May 1809.

Nearly 500 Frenchmen died of measles during their first winter on the moor. Typhus, smallpox, pneumonia and related diseases later killed hundreds of others, all of whom were buried in shallow pits on the open moor. The meagre diet; the overcrowded dormitories where the men were packed in hammocks side by side and one above the other as many as five high; the lack of heating arrangements and only wooden shutters over the windows to keep out the cold and the draught; the long wet winters with icy winds together with a lack of exercise over a period of more than six years took their toll on fit young men, most of whom were sailors. Altogether the French lost around 1250 men.

The French prisoners were later joined by Americans captured in the War of 1812. They were mostly sailors too. The 'Yankees' were in captivity for just over two years and consequently the numbers of their dead were lower but none the less tragic. Their casualties resulted from the same causes as the Frenchmen but to a lesser degree except for a smallpox epidemic

French POWs marching to Dartmoor Prison after Waterloo 1815 (From a painting by a Dartmoor Prison inmate)

which swept through their ranks with devastating effect in the last winter they spent there killing more than 200 of them. The total known number of fatalities among the American prisoners for the whole of their imprisonment stands at 271 but there could be more.

In 1866, by which time Dartmoor had been refurbished for the reception of convict prisoners, the remains of the dead prisoners of war were exhumed and reburied in two mass graves over each of which a cairn was erected surmounted by an obelisk. After 136 years both memorials were in need of renovation and this work has been handsomely done in the American cemetery with the French enclosure still in hand. On completion it is hoped arrangements will be made for the general public to visit.

The American Obelisk (Author's photo)

Among the victims of both nationalities were a number of suicides most of whom killed themselves in despair having deteriorated physically and mentally to the point of hopelessness. Even when their respective wars ended and with freedom at hand several prisoners were 'Found Hanged in the Prisons' or simply 'Found Dead' as the juries who presided over the inquests on them put it. Some French officers died in duels – the traditional (although illegal) method of settling their differences. Home-made swords with compass points or razors fixed to stout sticks were substitutes for real weapons and proved to be just as deadly in skilled hands. The lower ranks manufactured daggers with broken glass or nails embedded in wooden handles with which to settle their arguments, mainly gambling disputes. There was just one murder among the American prisoners and it was committed without using any weapons. Two seamen, Thomas Hill and James Henry both United States Navy men from the same ship (the 'Argus'), argued and fought with their fists when Henry was beaten so severely he died. The culprit was charged with manslaughter at Exeter Assize but the case could not be proved and he was acquitted and sent back to Dartmoor.

Homicide is a rare occurrence in British prisons these days but Dartmoor has the distinction of having had to deal with a vicious incident in which an inmate died a violent death. It happened in 1961 in the 'Old Chapel' where Church of England services were held and which was the venue for film shows and concerts. The details of this incident reveal the worst of Dartmoor prison 'culture' at that time. Out of 500 inmates twenty two were serving terms of life imprisonment, over 200 had ten to fifteen years to serve and a similar number were serving five and ten years; many of them were murderers and men convicted of violent offences.

In the afternoon of Sunday 11th June there was a film show (*The Blue Lamp*) during which a knife fight took place as a result of which one man died and another three were wounded. The dead man was thirty eight year old Harold Dennis Thirkettle, a native of Hull serving a twelve year sentence for manslaughter. He was killed by Matthew Nwachukwa, a Nigerian serving ten years for wounding, procuring and living on immoral earnings. The other two involved were Joseph Lane aged twenty eight, a Yorkshire man doing eight years for manslaughter, and thirty seven year old Thomas Williams, a Welshman with fourteen previous convictions.

The incident occurred during the final reel of the film when a disturbance alerted the officers who at once switched on the lights. Nwachukwa was standing on a pew holding other prisoners at bay with his arm raised and a knife in his hand dripping blood. Two officers managed to grab the knife and hustle him away to protect him from a large number of inmates threatening to kill him (he already had a knife wound in his back). Lane and Williams had serious knife wounds. Then Thirkettle was seen being carried by other prisoners who told the officers he had also been stabbed and this was found to be the case – three stab wounds to the chest, one of which had penetrated his heart. He died soon afterwards. The weapon came from the prison mat shop and had the word 'grass' scratched on the handle. It had been thrust into Nuwachuka's back and left there. The victim himself had managed to remove it and in a frenzy of fear stabbed all three wounded men sitting behind him in the belief it was one of them who carried out the attack (he had previously been tipped off he would be knifed because sex offenders were disliked).

70

Nuwachuka stood trial for manslaughter at Winchester Assizes, pleading not guilty on the grounds he had acted in self defence, and this was accepted by the Judge and Jury who found him 'Not Guilty'. No further charges were brought concerning the other two stabbings. Who stabbed Nuwachuka? Dartmoor prisoners would not talk openly about it neither would they give evidence but police officers heard enough from them 'off the record' to be convinced it was not the dead man who did it.

A runaway convict drowns

Very few prisoners have escaped from Dartmoor and remained at liberty. Most escapees never got out of the county and the ones who did were located sooner or later and returned to custody. Even fewer have died 'on the run' which is surprising when the dangerous conditions on the moor are taken into account, especially in the winter months with poorly clad men fumbling in the dark in unknown terrain among the bogs, gullies, and swift flowing rivers. Death from exposure comes to those who falter after getting wet or exhausted on the open moor and the risk of drowning is very real. One particular incident which occurred forty five years ago is still remembered by older residents in the Dartmoor area because the circumstances surrounding it were never (to their minds) satisfactorily explained.

The afternoon of 5th January 1959 experienced the very worst of Dartmoor weather. It was blowing a gale and lashing with rain with visibility down to a few yards due to a dense mist. One would have thought the inmates employed in the prison workshops were experiencing a rare sense of cheerfulness to be working inside in the relative comfort of their workplace. Two men however secretly welcomed the ferocious conditions out there because that is precisely where they planned to go. Dennis Stafford aged twenty five and thirty year old William Joseph Day were both seasoned criminals under extra surveillance at Dartmoor because of their previous escapes. Both were determined men who saw the atrocious weather as an ideal opportunity to put into effect an escape plan (which must have been arranged for some time) and the storm would shield them from their pursuers once they got clear of the prison.

The weak spot in security the two men were to take advantage of was the scaffolding adjacent to their workplace erected by contractors carrying out repairs to the roof. The official version of events tells of Stafford being excused to visit the lavatory where he was joined by Day. They somehow prised open the cast-iron window frame and shinned down the scaffolding so conveniently positioned outside, using a spare scaffold pole to clamber over the boundary wall to freedom. They were spotted as they went over the wall but quickly disappeared into the mist.

Tavistock police were alerted and tracker dogs were sent from Torquay to assist in the hunt for the two men but it was a hopeless task for the dogs as all traces of scent were obliterated by the pouring rain. Police and warders manning road blocks had to shout to make themselves heard above the roar of the wind and no-one had any idea which way the fugitives had gone. Local farmers were contacted by telephone and asked to search their barns and outhouses and report anything suspicious; that and reliance on the public who might spot something unusual was the best hope of obtaining a 'lead' as to the missing men's whereabouts.

A number of reports soon came their way. Residents at Dousland and Bickleigh rang to say they had heard footsteps outside their homes; a motorist told of seeing two men getting into a saloon car near Rundlestone just a short distance from the prison; a car was stolen from Plymouth and found abandoned after crashing near Horrabridge. These incidents were investigated and found not to be connected with the escapees. Then a car was stolen from Yelverton with a prison type mitten lying where the vehicle had been – the first real clue for the searchers and it afterwards proved to be authentic. It was driven to a town in Dorset and abandoned. Dennis Stafford was located and arrested in London on 20th February having been at large for forty seven days.

Back on Dartmoor a dramatic discovery took place eleven days after the escape when the body of Day was found in Burrator Reservoir by a passer-by. It was lying on the bottom not far from the dam and the circumstances surrounding his death may never be satisfactorily explained. Stafford was questioned after his recapture and maintained the pair of them had initially followed the obsolete railway track from Princetown and in the dark found themselves on a road skirting the reservoir when they saw headlights approaching. They scrambled over a fence to avoid being seen only to find themselves on a grass verge at the water's edge. He managed to grab a telegraph pole but his companion slipped and fell into the water shouting for help. He (Stafford) looked for and found a lifebelt but by the time he got back it was too late. He heard 'a gurgling sound' but did not see or hear Day again. His story was partly endorsed when it was recalled a lifebelt had been found floating in the reservoir.

What really happened? Day had previously escaped from Exeter prison

Burrator Reservoir (Courtesy Paul Rendell)

Dartmoor Prison today (Author's photo)

in June 1957 and was hunted for forty hours before being recaptured in dramatic fashion. During a pursuit near Crediton he had made for the River Yeo and was caught after completely submerging himself in the river and breathing through a hollow reed in true Hollywood film style. Was he attempting to do the same when he drowned, misjudging the depth of water perhaps? Some of his pursuers speculated Stafford might have accidentally or otherwise shoved him aside in his effort to save himself from falling in. Rumours spread that he had left Day to his fate and that the 'underworld' condemned him for it, which in turn led to information as to his whereabouts being passed to the police. Whatever took place that terrible night only two people knew the true facts and one of them is dead.

What about Stafford? He was already notorious, having escaped from Wormwood Scrubs in 1956 and making his way to Port of Spain in the West Indies where he was discovered and sent back to England and to Dartmoor. In later life he was implicated in a murder and found guilty – the details of the case formed the basis of the film *Get Carter* starring Michael Caine. He served two more terms of imprisonment and was recommended for parole but the decision was overruled by the Home Secretary. In May 2002 the European Court of Human Rights awarded Stafford a total of £28,365 in damages and legal costs for being illegally detained longer then the Parole Board recommendation. Today he lives quietly in the North of England under an assumed name.

The Policeman's View

When I read the various accounts of the treatment of the prisoners of war held at Dartmoor during the course of various conflicts I can't help but be ashamed at the hypocrisy with which we look upon our 'glorious' history. The unhygienic and brutal conditions in which the prisoners were kept would have instigated an outcry if British prisoners had been subjected to such treatment. At last a fitting memorial has been raised to those poor souls whose only crime was to serve their nations in times of war. Having a strong sense of justice makes me wonder at how those captives were treated compared with those of later years in the convict jail.

The case of Stafford and Day is one which might make the general public question the rights and wrongs of our judicial system. We will only ever have Stafford's account to explain the death of his companion Day. Some might consider that when his 'day of reckoning' comes a thorough investigation will be conducted by the Highest of all Authorities. I know that this view is one shared by my friend Ken Northey. It was he, as a local police constable, who pulled the lifeless body of Day from Burrator Reservoir. I know that he too wonders at the events leading up to his death. Some might think it reasonable to perhaps allow oneself a cynical smile at a judicial system that awards a man such as Stafford a fortune in these circumstances. I know this is not the first time I have had such shameful thoughts.

Some years ago during a bad winter I recaptured an escaping convict from the marshes at the head of the River Walkham to where I had chased him. He was in a hypothermic state after we had both got quite a soaking. I took him to Tavistock Hospital for care and attention whilst I had to sit outside in the cold! Such is life I thought and such is 'justice' – long may it continue!

Constable Simon Dell., MBE., QCB.

Acknowlegements.
Police Sergeant K. Northey (Rtd.).
Constable Simon Dell, MBE., QCB.
Mr. David Worth, Princetown.
Dartmoor Prisoner of War Depot and Convict Jail by Trevor James (Orchard Publications 2002).
Western Morning News (Plymouth).
Tavistock Gazette.

A STORY OF THREE LIVES

The First.

Of all the commercial undertakings on Dartmoor mining has been the most lucrative and extensive. The remains of the tinner's work are everywhere to be seen – man made gulleys, pits and spoil heaps, leats, blowing houses and so on, not to mention the occasional engine house chimney adjacent to the defunct and rusty equipment which was used to break up and separate the precious metal from the diggings. Immeasurable wealth was generated from mediaeval times to the 20th. century by an army of workers, many of whom lived on the moor a week at a time bringing food to last until Saturday finish, sleeping and eating their frugal fare in stone huts whose ruins are also visible over the landscape. They were tough hard-living men who literally tore the area apart in their quest for tin, copper, lead, zinc, and other ores, but success came at a terrible price in lives lost or shortened by the hardships and dangers associated with their work, especially those who toiled underground.

The late 'Gillie' Warne of Princetown is believed to have been the last tin miner on Dartmoor, working at Birch Tor (near Warren House Inn) as a young man. He died in August 2000 aged eighty nine years – which reminds

Miners preparing a hole for blasting (Courtesy Paul Rendell)

us that the turbulent mining era has only just passed from living memory.

In 1882 the busiest mining operations on Dartmoor took place in the Birch Tor area near Warren House on the Two Bridges – Moretonhampstead road. Golden Dagger tin mine, owned and operated by Mr. Moses Bawden of Tavistock, was close by (the ruins are still visible today) and it was here a horrifying accident occurred in February of that year.

Richard Stephens and John Webb were working together underground on what was known as the 'tribute' system, the equivalent of 'piece work' today whereby the men were paid a fixed sum for every ton of ore delivered at the surface. The usual and quickest method of working under this system was by 'stoping' which entailed hacking and blasting their way upwards from the levels so that the loosened material fell to the floor in pieces which could be removed more easily than by having to work around it as would be the case if working horizontally. Tribute work also encouraged haste and economy on safety, which was to prove fatal for Mr. Stephens who was engaged in the blasting. This was done using 'black powder' (gunpowder) a quantity of which was inserted into a hole made in the rock and tightly sealed with 'wadding' made of either clay or coarse decomposed granite, the latter being an acknowledged substitute on Dartmoor where clay was unobtainable (this practice ensured the force of the explosion was directed into the rock to break it up). A length of safety fuse would have previously been inserted in the hole with the charge so that it could be detonated from a safe distance. Stephens used a granite mix but instead of ramming it home with a wooden tamping rod or 'stemmer' he inserted the iron bar he had made the hole with (it saved a minute or so of time in exchanging it for the wooden rod) and despite a warning from his mate struck it with a mallet.

An explosion shook the mine and Stephens received the full force of it with terrible consequences – his head was opened up so that his brains were exposed and eyes shockingly injured. A man was immediately sent to Moretonhampstead for medical assistance but this was rejected by no less than three doctors: local practitioner Mr. Collings was expecting two confinements and could not come. An urgent message was then sent to Mr. Hunt of Chagford who failed to turn up. In desperation Mr. May of Moretonhampstead was approached but as well as stating he too was awaiting a confinement case he would not attend until he received his fee.

Miner Richard Stephens died from his injuries and we will never know if prompt medical attention could have saved him. He had disobeyed written instructions openly displayed by his employers not to use iron or steel tamping rods for ramming. Gunpowder is 'spark sensitive' and either the iron bar in contact with the granite wadding created a spark or the rod, which it will be remembered was struck with a mallet, came up against the powder itself and could have caused the explosion.

At an Inquest held three days later the Coroner in his summing up not only expressed the hope that the accident would deter others from using an iron bar as the deceased had done, but thought that 'a gentleman who objected to attend such a case unless he received a fee was an exception to the grand rule of the medical profession to attend cases regardless of fees'. In returning a verdict of 'Accidental Death' the Jury also expressed their regret at Mr. May's conduct. 'A LIFE THROWN AWAY THROUGH CARELESSNESS' was the headline of a newspaper report of the proceedings.

The Second

A doctor who would not attend a patient unless he first received his fee deserved to be reprimanded but in Victorian England the majority of ordinary folk simply could not afford to seek his services anyway. For paupers, the aged and infirm, or the mentally unfit there was only the workhouse to go to – a bitter last resort and dreaded by all. It was also the only refuge for that piteous object of scorn at that time – the unmarried mother. Young women who found themselves 'in trouble' were often disowned by their families and dismissed to fend for themselves. Many a girl in this situation faced a life of hopeless poverty and isolation with the workhouse her only 'home'. In some institutions they were compelled to wear yellow clothing to distinguish them from their more 'respectable' companions.

On Wednesday 18th May 1870 John Giles, a farmer from Bickleigh, near Plymouth, was driving sheep over Roborough Down when he saw a young woman with a baby in her arms walking along the turnpike road from the Tavistock direction. She was Mary Ann Trewin, a twenty two years old unmarried mother and former servant girl who had tramped all the way from Tavistock Union Workhouse where she had given birth to a baby girl a month previously. On her departure the workhouse nurse asked where she would go and the mother said she had friends at Buckland (presumably she meant Buckland Monachorum near Yelverton) who would care for the child, after which she would go back to her old employers, a farming family who lived not far from that place. Mr. Giles saw her turn off the highway into a lane leading to the hamlet of Clearbrook. A short time later Mary arrived alone at the house of a friend in Clearbrook, Ann Hatherleigh, who evidently knew

Tavistock Union Workhouse now Russell Court, an attractive development of residential flats (Author's photo)

The 'Skylark Inn' at Clearbrook – a very old picture (Courtesy Paul Rendell)

about her circumstances and asked about the new born baby. The child had died and was buried the previous Saturday she was told.

Two days later, Friday 20th May, Mr. Samuel Luscombe, who was employed as a maintenance worker on the Devonport Leat (which crossed Roborough Down a short distance away) discovered the corpse of a child lying on the bank. He covered the body with furze and went to the police station at Roborough where he reported his find. Police Sergeant Butt took charge and went with Mr. Luscombe to recover the body. He had obviously made enquiries and found out where the child had come from and who the mother was because he then proceeded to the Skylark Inn at Clearbrook to ask after Miss Trewin. She was staying at the home of Mr. and Mrs. Lillicrap where she had lived for a short time before going to the Union Workhouse.

When questioned by Sgt. Butt the mother repeated her story that her baby had died in the workhouse and was buried. The policeman then challenged her as to what her answer would be if he contacted the Master there to enquire whether or not a child had died and been buried as she claimed. When she made no reply she was taken into custody and charged with murdering her baby daughter.

On Tuesday 24th May an Inquest was held at Roborough Police Court before Mr. W.C. Radcliffe. Mr. Willis, the surgeon who performed a post mortem examination on the dead child, said as a result of his findings it was his belief the baby had been drowned. Maria Palmer, the nurse at the Tavistock Union Workhouse, gave evidence of the circumstances of the birth, stating the mother had been admitted to the workhouse on 21st December; she also identified the deceased as being the offspring of Miss Trewin. After listening to the Coroner's summing up the jury returned a verdict of 'Wilful Murder' against the mother.

Mary Ann Trewin was brought before Roborough Police Court on Wednesday 25th May charged with the murder of her six weeks old daughter and committed for trial at the next Assizes after saying nothing in her defence. At the Assize the jury found her guilty of a reduced charge of manslaughter and she received a sentence of seven years penal servitude.

The Third Life
Was that of Mary herself, who was fortunate not to have been hanged for murder – but her life was 'lost' just the same. She may have been seduced by someone in the household where she worked and lived, a not uncommon occurrence in those days; in any case boyfriends were either discouraged or

banned outright on pain of dismissal by many employers. The young woman must have been discharged when her pregnancy became known for her to have sought refuge in the workhouse in the first place – just days before Christmas. Killing an infant was always regarded as the most vile of crimes and having been convicted of causing the death of a child her time spent in prison among the worst female criminals in the land would have been harrowing in the extreme. Picking oakum* or winding a crank a set number of turns each day to earn her keep together with the effects of a frugal diet would have left their mark upon her physically and mentally. On her release, with no references, no friends, no home and a reputation in ruins, what hope had she of ever again holding a position of trust? In the comfort and security of our modern age a more liberal approach exists for those who 'fall by the wayside' and who but the most heartless among us can feel anything other than some sympathy for Mary Ann Trewin, a poor girl who acted against all her maternal instincts possibly from panic and certainly from despair?

Her story is a sad reflection on what many of us now regard as the obsessive moral scruples of Victorian times and is a vivid contrast to the understanding and help shown today even when such benevolence is looked upon by some as being too liberal and compassionate.

* A process whereby a length of tarred rope (hard as iron) was reduced to a pile of fluffy strands by picking at it with the fingers. A fixed amount by weight was expected each day. The material produced was used to seal the joints between the planks on the decks of ships.

The Policeman's View

Having worked as a policeman in the tin mining area of west Cornwall I know all too well the hardships and privations suffered by the 20th Century tin miner. I have conducted too many investigations on behalf of H.M.Coroner into deaths attributed to this hazardous occupation to have nothing but the utmost respect for these men. I am sure they would agree that their mining forebears of one hundred years ago encountered far more dangers and risks of being killed on a regular basis. They even named one of their machines 'The Widow Maker', such were the dangers accepted as part of the job. My colleague at that time had been a tin miner like his father and grandfather before him and his stories filled me with admiration for these men - but he had chosen the 'softer' life of being a policeman above ground.

Richard Stephens may well have ignored the official rule of only using a wooden rod to 'tamp' the black powder, but he was working under great pressure to produce ore. I imagine these rules were broken daily and we must not regard his as an isolated and reckless case; men cut corners then, as we often do now when 'the management' is conveniently 'looking the other way'. I have seen many reports of similar accidents in mining and quarrying so the practice was not uncommon. I doubt if his life could have been saved if the doctor had come quickly but do not think ill of this hard working miner - he and men like him moulded the history and heritage of Dartmoor with their bare hands and we owe them much.

As for the unfortunate Mary Trewin, the unmarried mother of the murdered infant, she suffered the hypocrisy and prejudice that sometimes makes us feel ashamed of our great Victorian age. I do not condemn her for her actions; she was the product of the cruel and barbaric society into which she bore her child. Her name suggests that she may have come from a Cornish home many miles away and was alone in the world. When she was seen walking towards Clearbrook had she been turned away from her only hope of salvation at Buckland? Was she in such a state of desperation that she committed the greatest crime any mother could commit?

It is not for us to judge poor Mary, but to give thanks that the Workhouse system (which perhaps was responsible for committing the greater crime) is a thing of the past.

PC Simon Dell MBE., QCB

Acknowledgements:
Camborne School of Mines (University of Exeter), Redruth, Cornwall.
Constable Simon Dell MBE., QMB.
Mr. David Worth, Princetown.
Tavistock Gazette.